GARFIELD'S
FURRY·TALES

Created by
JIM DAVIS

Illustrated by Mike Fentz

Watermill Press

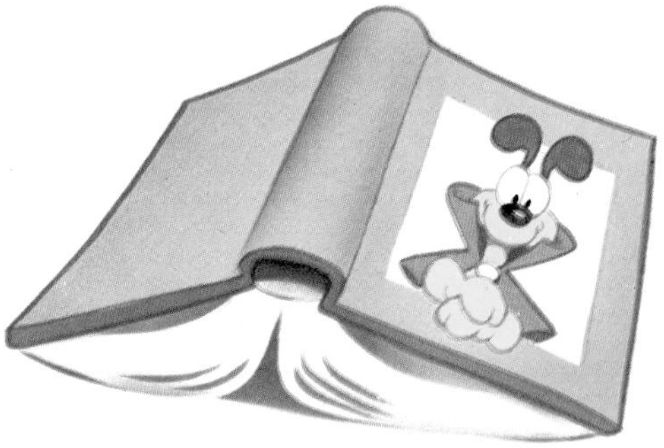

Published by Watermill Press, an imprint of Troll Associates, Inc.
Library of Congress Catalog Card Number: 88-80203

Printed in the United States of America.
10 9 8 7 6 5 4 3 2

Contents

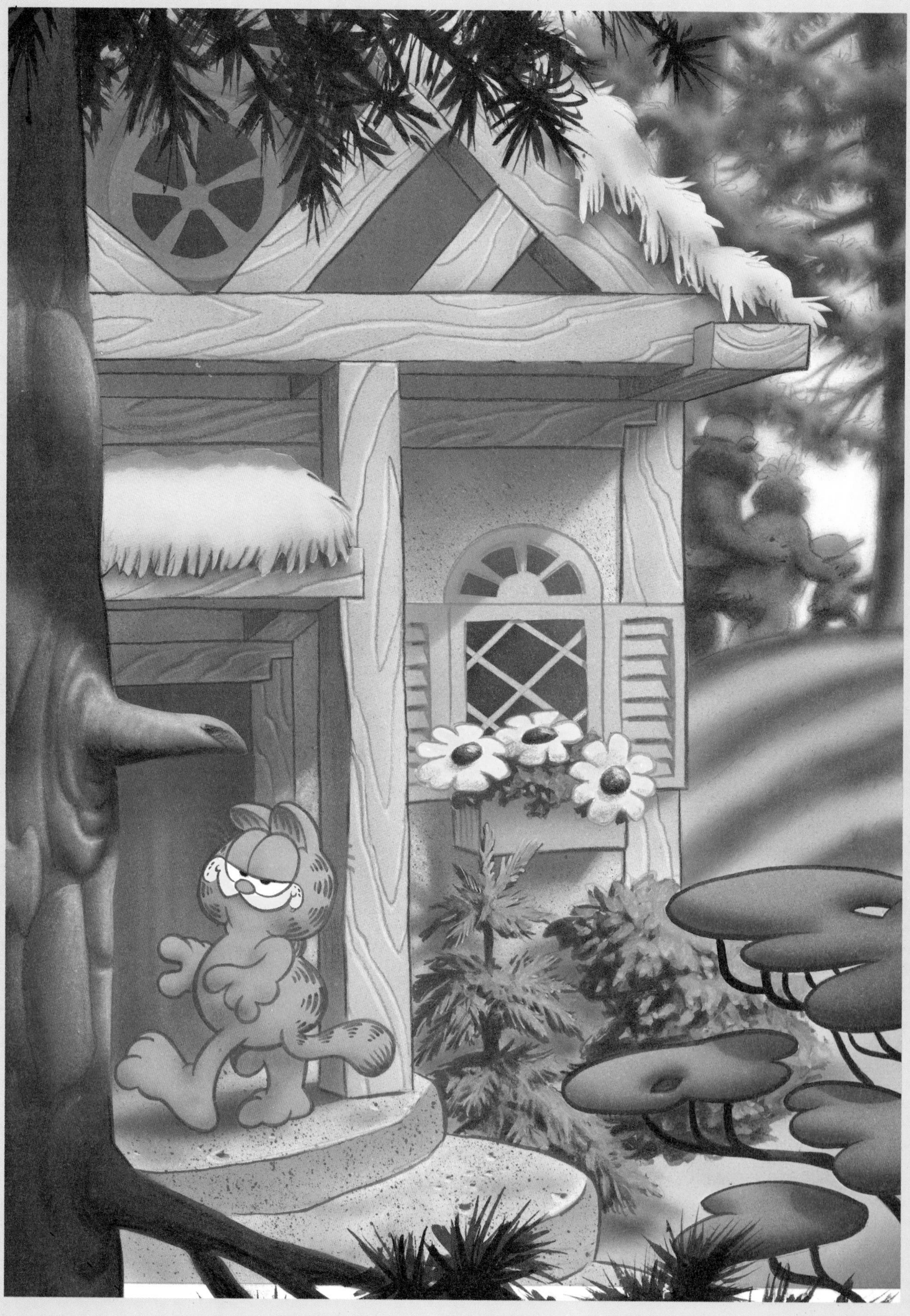

Garfield and the Three Bears

Once upon a time in a little cottage in the big woods lived three bears. There was great big Papa Bear, middle-sized Mama Bear, and itsy-bitsy Baby Bear.

One evening they sat down to a big lasagna dinner. Mama Bear said, "This lasagna is too hot. Let's go for a walk until it cools." So the three bears went out into the woods.

At the same time in the same woods, Jon was getting dinner ready for Garfield, Odie, and himself. Jon had dragged Garfield along on a camping trip, and Garfield was miserable. He was tired of eating hot dogs and sleeping on the hard ground. So he wandered away from the campsite, hoping to find a motel and decent food. But he had been walking in the woods for a long time, and all he had found was more woods.

"I'm beat," said Garfield, rubbing his tired feet. "Right now I'd be willing to sleep in a bears' cottage, as long as it's nicely decorated." Just then he spied the cottage of the three bears. "I had a feeling this was going to happen," he said.

Garfield knocked on the door of the cottage, but no one answered. So Garfield, being a curious and very tired cat, simply opened the door and walked in.

Inside was a table set with three plates of lasagna. There was a great big plate, a middle-sized plate, and an itsy-bitsy plate.

Garfield looked at the great big plate of lasagna. "Too small," he said. Then he looked at the middle-sized plate of lasagna. "Much too small," he said. Then he looked at the itsy-bitsy plate of lasagna. "You've got to be kidding," he said.

So he took all three plates of lasagna and dumped them into the pan in which the lasagna had been cooked. He gobbled up all the lasagna plus everything else in the three bears' refrigerator, except some liver and an old box of baking soda. Garfield patted his full tummy. "That should hold me until suppertime," he said.

In the living room Garfield saw a great big chair, a middle-sized chair, and an itsy-bitsy chair. Garfield tried the great big chair. "Too hard," he said. Then he sat in the middle-sized chair. "Too soft," he said. Finally he sat in the itsy-bitsy chair—and squashed it flat. "Too bad," said Garfield. "I hope they won't add this to my bill."

Garfield decided that what he really needed was a nap. He went into the bedroom. There he found a great big bed, a middle-sized bed, and an itsy-bitsy bed. "I'm beginning to see a pattern here," said Garfield.

He lay down on the great big bed. "This is nice," he said. Next he tried the middle-sized bed. "This is also nice," he said. Finally he tried the itsy-bitsy bed, which fortunately was stronger than the itsy-bitsy chair. "This is also very nice," said Garfield. "Which one should I choose?" He decided to start with a short nap in the itsy-bitsy bed.

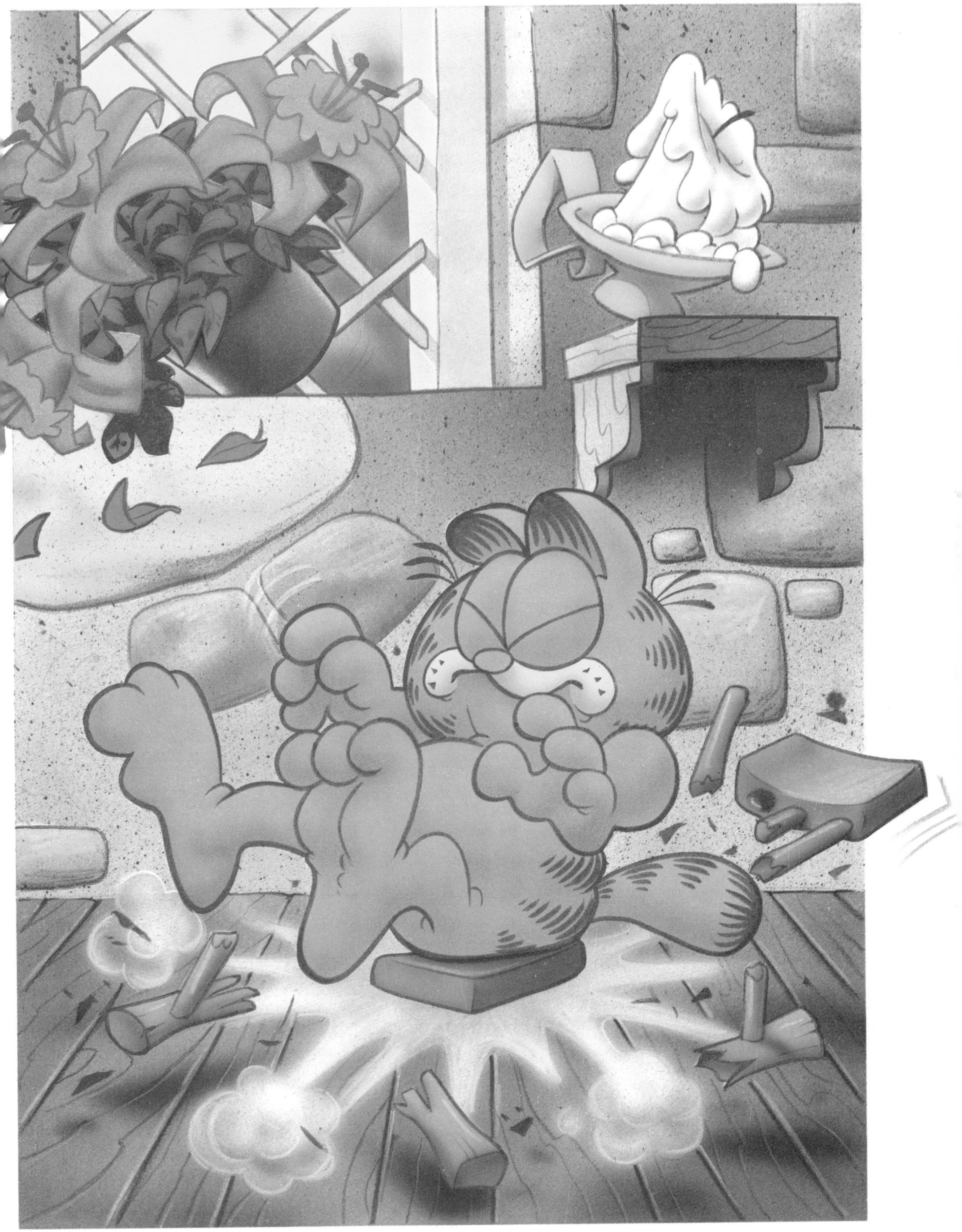

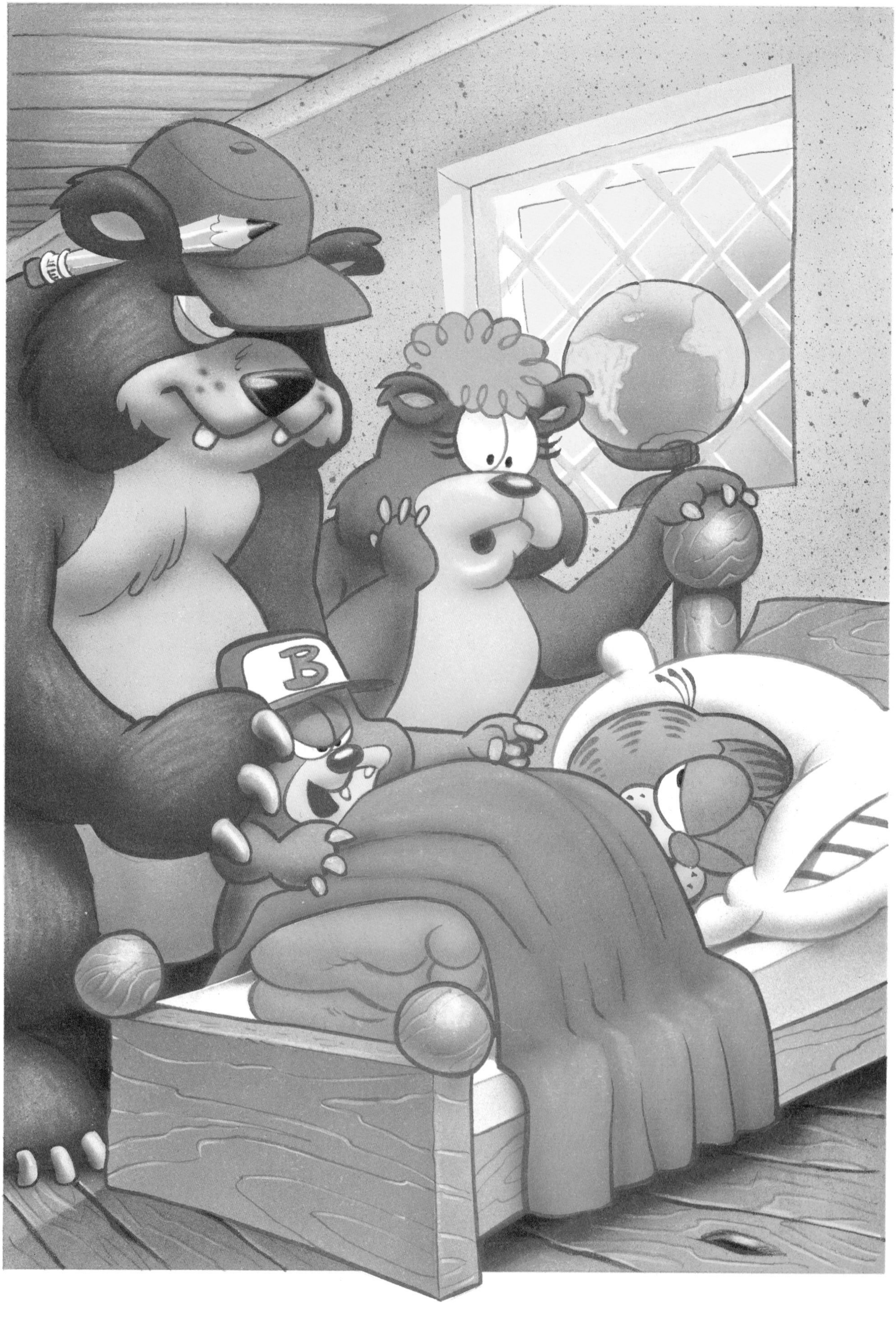
B

Soon afterward the three bears came home, feeling tired from their walk.

"We walked too long and too far," said Mama Bear. "Now our lasagna is going to be cold."

But their lasagna wasn't cold. It was gone!

"Someone's been eating my lasagna!" said great big Papa Bear in his great big voice.

"Someone's been eating my lasagna!" said middle-sized Mama Bear in her middle-sized voice.

"Someone's been eating my lasagna!" said itsy-bitsy Baby Bear in his itsy-bitsy voice. "And he cleaned out the refrigerator!"

The three bears quickly checked out the living room.

"Someone's been sitting in my chair!" said great big Papa Bear.

"Someone's been sitting in my chair!" said middle-sized Mama Bear.

"Someone's been sitting in my chair!" said itsy-bitsy Baby Bear. "And he squashed it flat!"

"Well, that's not surprising," said Mama Bear, "after eating all that lasagna!"

Finally the three bears crept cautiously into the bedroom. Great big Papa Bear picked something off his bed. "Someone left cat hair on my bed!" he said.

Middle-sized Mama Bear looked at her bed. "Someone left cat hair on my bed!" she said.

Itsy-bitsy Baby Bear looked at his itsy-bitsy bed. "Someone left cat hair on my bed!" he said. "And there's a fat cat still wearing it!"

Garfield sleepily opened one eye. "I'm sorry, but this room is taken," he said. "You three will have to stay somewhere else."

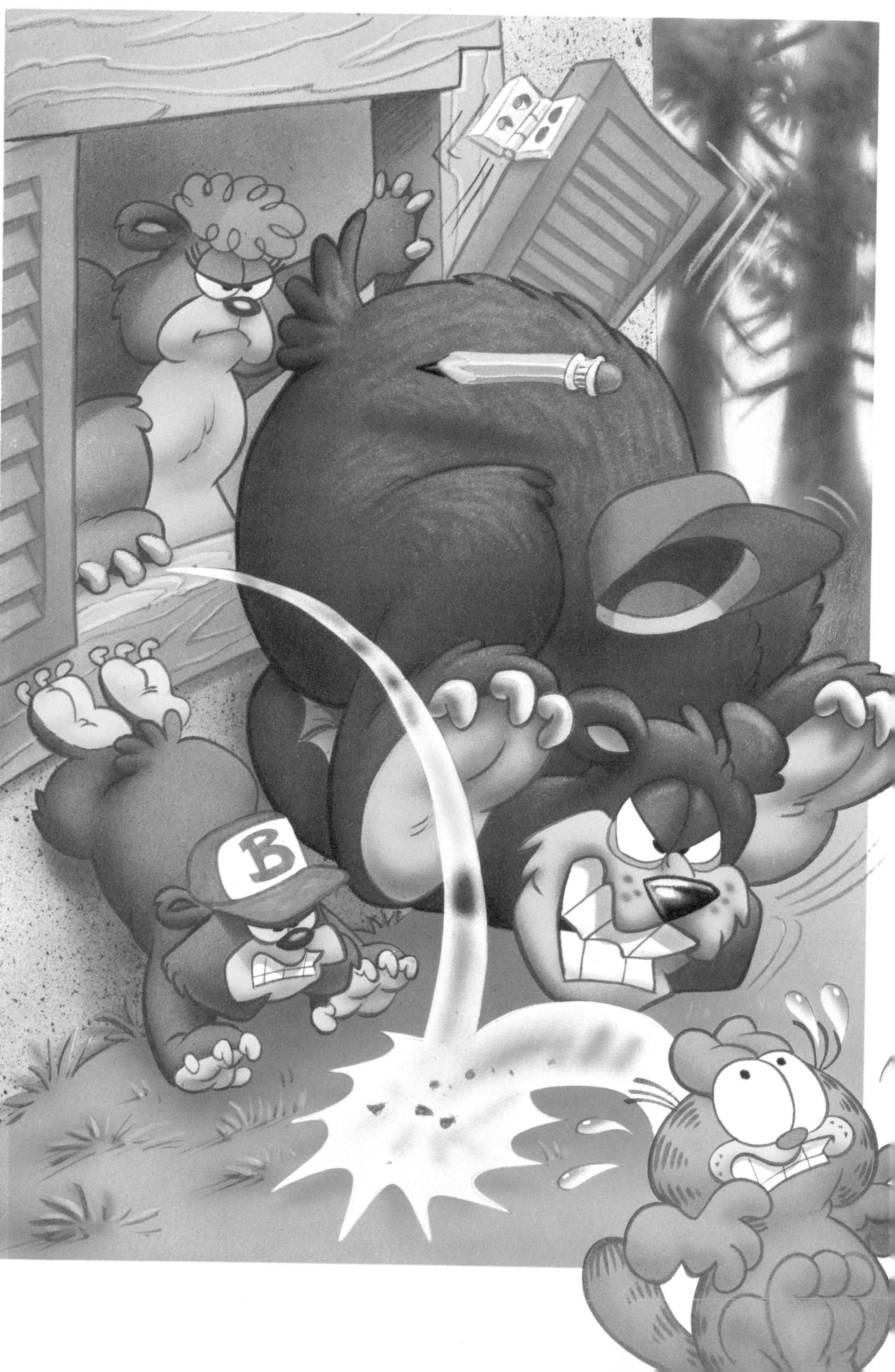

"Did you forget to lock the door again?" said middle-sized Mama Bear to great big Papa Bear. "This is just like the time with that little girl!"

"You're the elephant who broke my chair!" said itsy-bitsy Baby Bear to Garfield.

Now Garfield was wide awake. "I cannot sleep with all this noise," he said. "If you don't leave right now, I'm going to complain to the owners."

"We *are* the owners!" the three bears cried out.

"I'll be going now," said Garfield. And with that, he bolted from the bed, raced across the floor, and jumped out the window, with the three angry bears roaring at his heels.

Garfield ran faster than he ever had before, and he soon left the bears far behind. Huffing and puffing, he sat down on a log to rest. "That's the last time I stay at that place," he said. "The food wasn't bad, but the bears weren't the least bit friendly."

After he caught his breath, Garfield began walking again, and he soon found Jon and Odie. Garfield spent the rest of the camping trip complaining about the food and the hard ground, but he never went far from camp.

The bears, of course, had to eat liver for supper that night. And the next day great big Papa Bear put up a great big sign that said NO CATS ALLOWED!

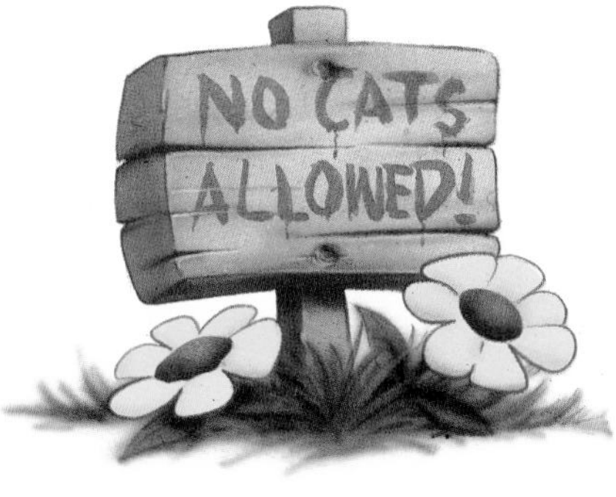
NO CATS
ALLOWED!

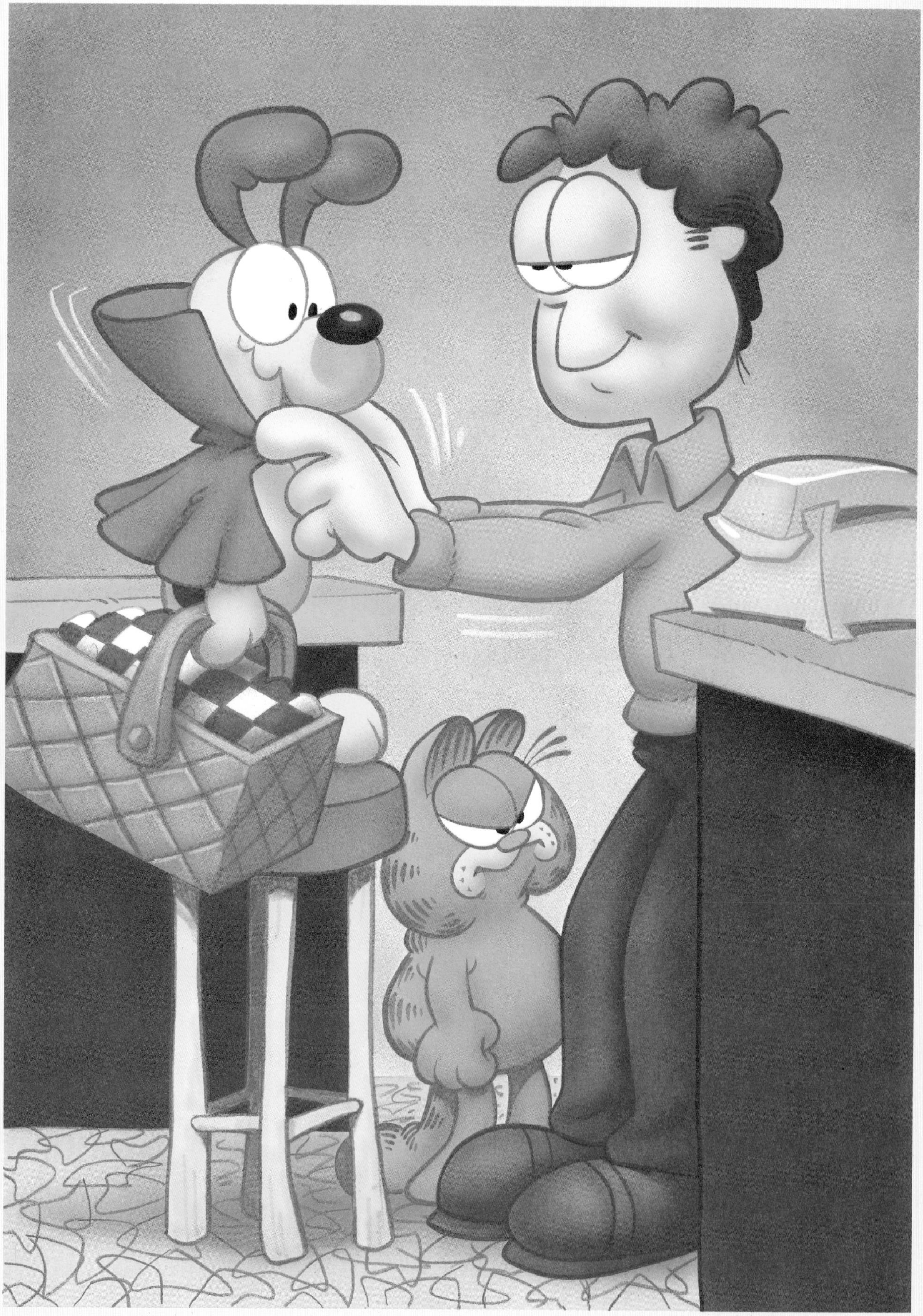

Little Red Riding Odie

It was one of Garfield's favorite times of the year—Girl Scout cookie time. Jon had placed a huge order with the Girl Scout next door, and the shipment had just arrived. Garfield eyed the boxes of cookies hungrily, trying to decide which tempting package he should attack first.

Just then Garfield heard Jon talking on the phone. "I'm sorry to hear about your cold, Grandma," said Jon. "But I know what will make you feel better. I'll send Odie over with a big basket of Girl Scout cookies."

Garfield was shocked. "What kind of grandson sends cookies to his sick grandmother?" he asked himself. "She can have my orange juice. She can have my chicken soup. But if she thinks she's getting any of my Girl Scout cookies, she'd better think again!"

Garfield watched Jon hand a big basket of Girl Scout cookies to Odie. "This is a very simple job," said Jon.

"Simple jobs for simple dogs," said Garfield.

"Just take this basket of cookies to Grandma's," Jon continued. "I'd send you-know-who, but the cookies would never get there. Take the shortcut through the woods. And wear this red cape, because it's cold outside."

"And besides, that's how the story goes," said Garfield.

So Odie set off through the woods for Grandma's house. Little did he know what surprise lay ahead. For just as he rounded a bend in the path, there was Garfield leaning against a tree.

"Odie, old pal," said Garfield.

"Arf!" barked Odie in surprise.

"I'm so glad I caught you," said Garfield. "Just after you left, Grandma called to say she was moving to Florida. So she won't need those cookies after all."

"Arf?" said Odie, confused as usual.

"That basket must be heavy," said Garfield. "Why not let me carry it home for you?" He reached for the basket.

"Grrrr," said Odie.

Garfield stepped back. "Why, Odie, don't you trust me?"

"Arf!" said Odie as he slipped around Garfield and raced away down the path.

"I hate it when that dumb dog shows signs of intelligence," said Garfield, racing after Odie.

By using an even shorter shortcut, Garfield reached Grandma's house ahead of Odie. "Now, all I need to do is find a way to get Granny out of the house," thought Garfield. In an instant he came up with a plan.

He rang Grandma's doorbell. "Why, Garfield! What a nice surprise!" said Grandma as she opened the door. Garfield's face took on a look of panic, and he began breathing hard. He jumped up and down, waving his arms and pointing back in the direction he had come.

"What is it, Garfield?" asked Grandma. "What's wrong? It's Jon, isn't it? There's something wrong with Jon. Oh, dear!"

"I'm going to hate myself for this in the morning," said Garfield, and he continued to act upset.

14

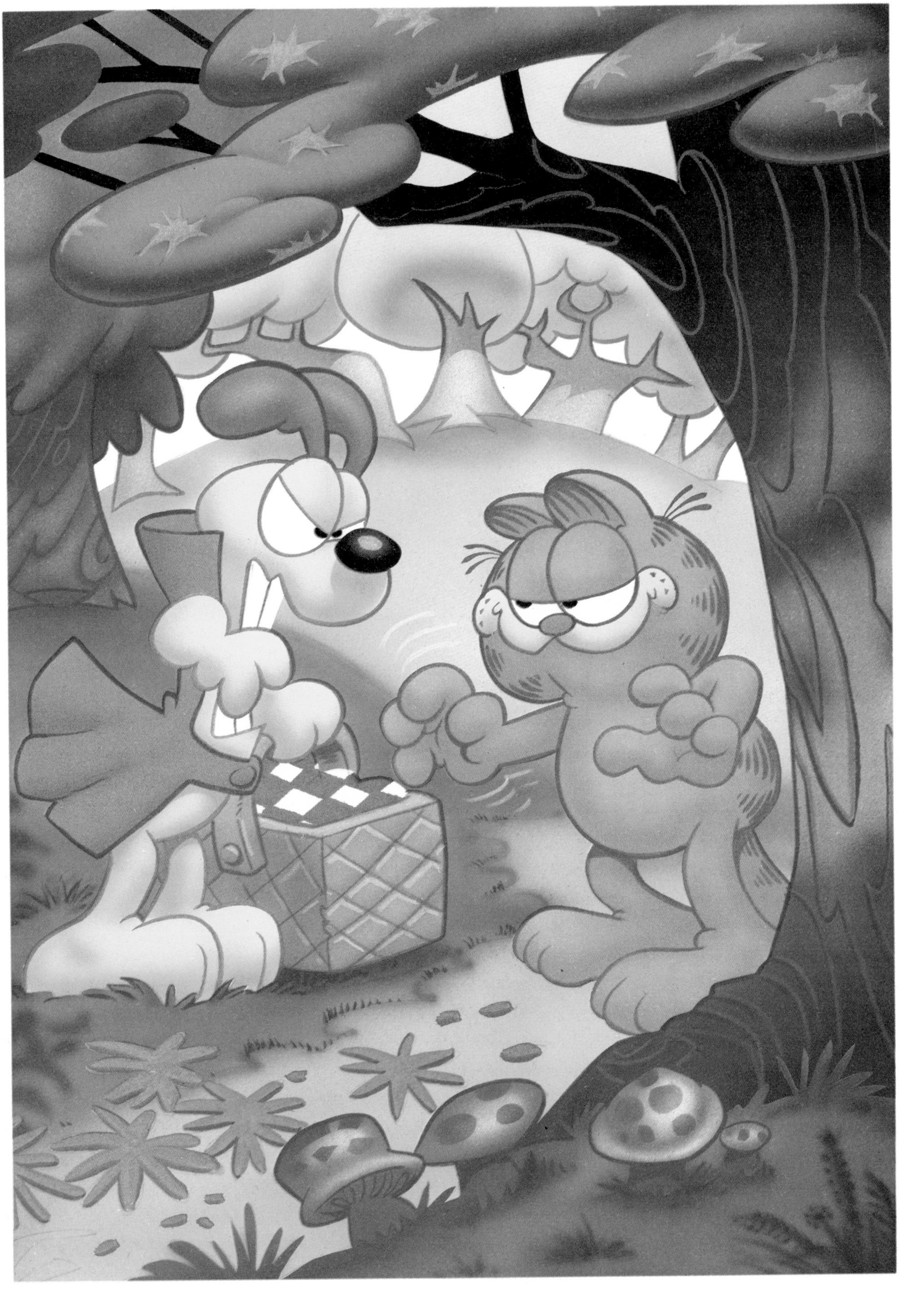

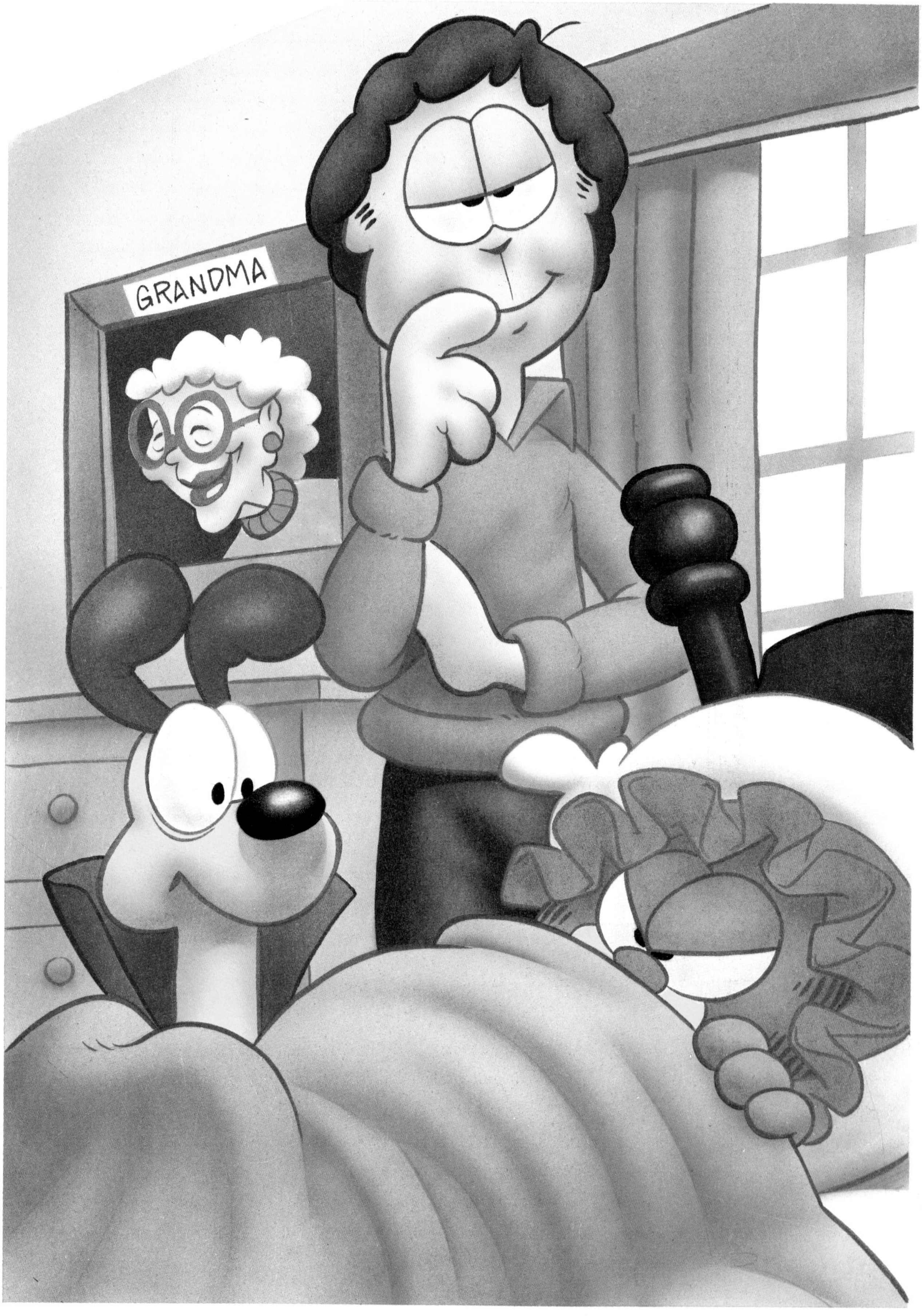
GRANDMA

"Sick or not, I must go to Jon," said Grandma. She grabbed her hat and purse, jumped into her car, and sped away.

"Don't forget to write," said Garfield, waving to her. "And now, to complete my plan," he thought, hopping into the house.

In a flash Garfield put on one of Grandma's nightcaps and nightgowns and jumped into her bed. He pulled the covers up to his nose. And not a minute too soon, for Odie stuck his head inside the door.

"Cough, cough, wheeze, sniffle," said Garfield. Odie made a sad face and hopped over to the bed. Setting down the basket, he gave Garfield a big fat lick.

"Yech!" thought Garfield. "That's enough to make anybody sick." He pulled the covers up to his eyes. "How sweet of you to bring those cookies for me," said Garfield. "Now, hand them over."

Just then, Jon came through the door.

"Rats!" said Garfield.

"Why, Grandma," said Jon, "you look absolutely terrible."

"I'm sick. What's your excuse?" said Garfield.

"And what big eyes you have," said Jon.

"The better to keep an eye on my Girl Scout Cookies," said Garfield.

"And what big ears you have, Granny," said Jon.

"The better to overhear your dumb plans," said Garfield.

"And look at those big teeth!" said Jon.

"The better for cookie munching," said Garfield.

"And Grandma," said Jon, "what an enormous fat tummy you have!"

"Watch it!" said Garfield.

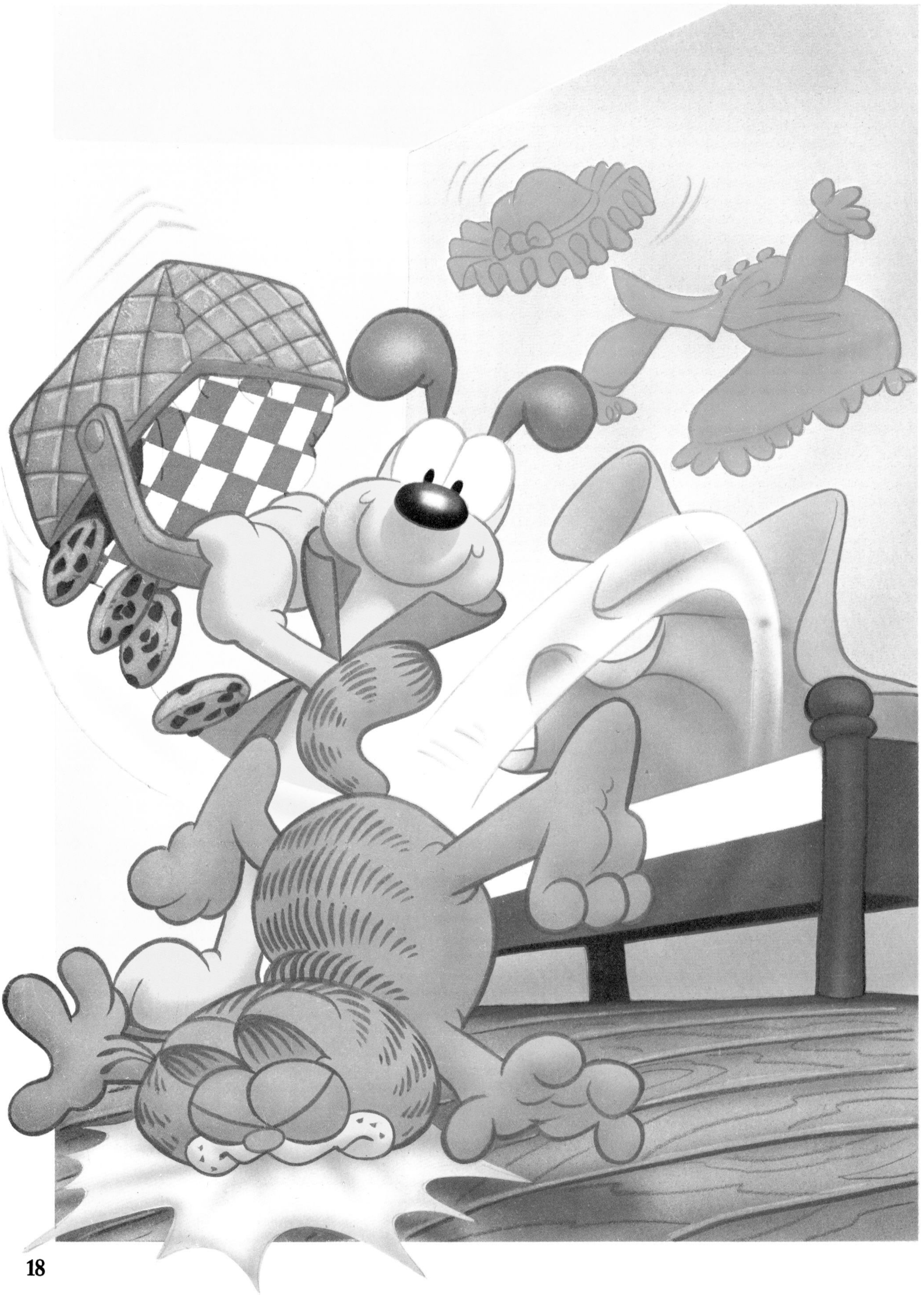

"In fact," said Jon, patting Garfield's tummy, "I think maybe you're sick because you're so out of shape. What you need is exercise, not cookies. Odie and I will just eat them ourselves."

Moving as fast as a fat cat can move, Garfield lunged for the cookie basket. But Odie snatched it away, so that all Garfield got was a face full of floor.

"Aha!" shouted Jon. "We knew it was you all the time, didn't we, Odie?"

"Arf?" said Odie.

"When I couldn't find you at home, Garfield," said Jon, "I knew you were up to something tricky. So I got here as fast as I could. Did you really think you could get away with this?"

"It almost worked for the wolf," said Garfield. "I figured I could do better."

"But what happened to Grandma?" asked Jon.

Just then they heard a car pull up in front of the house.

"Jon!" shouted Grandma. "You're all right!"

"Grandma!" shouted Jon. "*You're* all right!"

All eyes fixed on Garfield.

"Don't look at me," he said. "I was just doing what everybody expected me to. Now, when do we eat?"

Grandma decided that since there were so many cookies, even Garfield could have some. So they all lived happily ever after . . . at least until the cookies ran out.

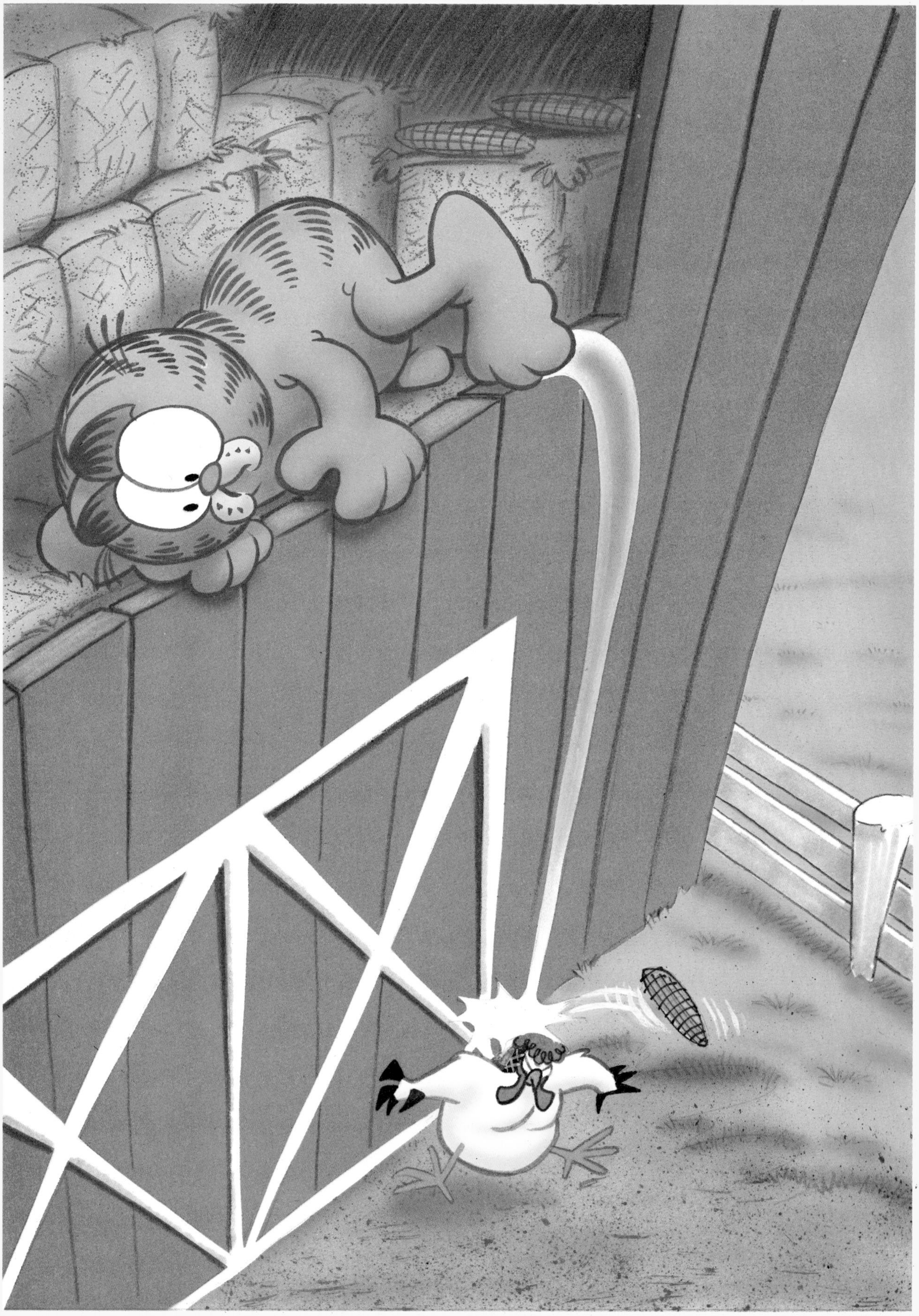

Garfield and Penny Henny

Whenever Garfield visited Jon's parents' farm, he spent a lot of time up in the hayloft. It was a great place to enjoy a view of the beautiful countryside. It was a great place to eat without being seen. Best of all, it was a great place to take a nap without being disturbed.

But one afternoon, while Garfield was trying to nap, he heard a loud "Cluck, cluck, cluck." Looking down at the farmyard, he saw the hen known as Penny Henny, clucking at nothing in particular. Turning over in the loft, he accidentally kicked a corn-on-the-cob, and it fell right on the hen's head.

Garfield quickly scampered down the ladder to the barnyard. The hen was shaking her head and looking up in amazement at the clear blue sky.

"What happened?" asked Garfield, pretending innocence.

"I don't know," said Penny Henny. "I was just walking along, scratching the dirt for grubs, when suddenly something dropped out of the sky onto my head!"

"Gee, I hope that doesn't mean that the sky is falling," Garfield said slyly.

"Oh, my goodness!" said the astonished Penny Henny. "That must be it! The sky is falling! The sky is falling!"

"This chicken has all the brains of a rock—or worse still, a dog," thought Garfield. He decided to see how far the joke would go.

Garfield said, "If the sky is falling—and I'm not saying it is, although that's the only way to explain it—then don't you think someone should warn the rest of the world?"

"Oh, you're absolutely right," said Penny Henny. "I must go and warn everyone." With that, she ran off to give the news to the other animals. Garfield followed her. "This is almost too easy," he thought.

Penny Henny raced up to Rusty Rooster. "The sky is falling! The sky is falling!" she cried. "We must warn the other animals!"

Rusty Rooster looked up at the sky. "I don't see anything," he said.

"Well, it hit me on the head," said Penny Henny.

"It's probably only bits and pieces falling right now," said Garfield. "But any minute the roof could cave in."

"Let's get out of here!" said Rusty Rooster, covering his head with his wings.

"What do you know?" said Garfield to himself. "Stupidity is contagious."

The next animal they met was Chucky Ducky. "The sky is falling!" cried Rusty Rooster. "A piece the size of a car hit Penny Henny on the head."

"She looks all right to me," said Chucky Ducky, confused.

"Well, she's a plucky little chicken," said Rusty Rooster. "I was very lucky not to be hit myself."

"Are you sure about this?" asked Chucky Ducky.

"A duck on the next farm was hit, too," said Garfield.

"Really?" said Chucky Ducky.

"All they found was his bill," said Garfield.

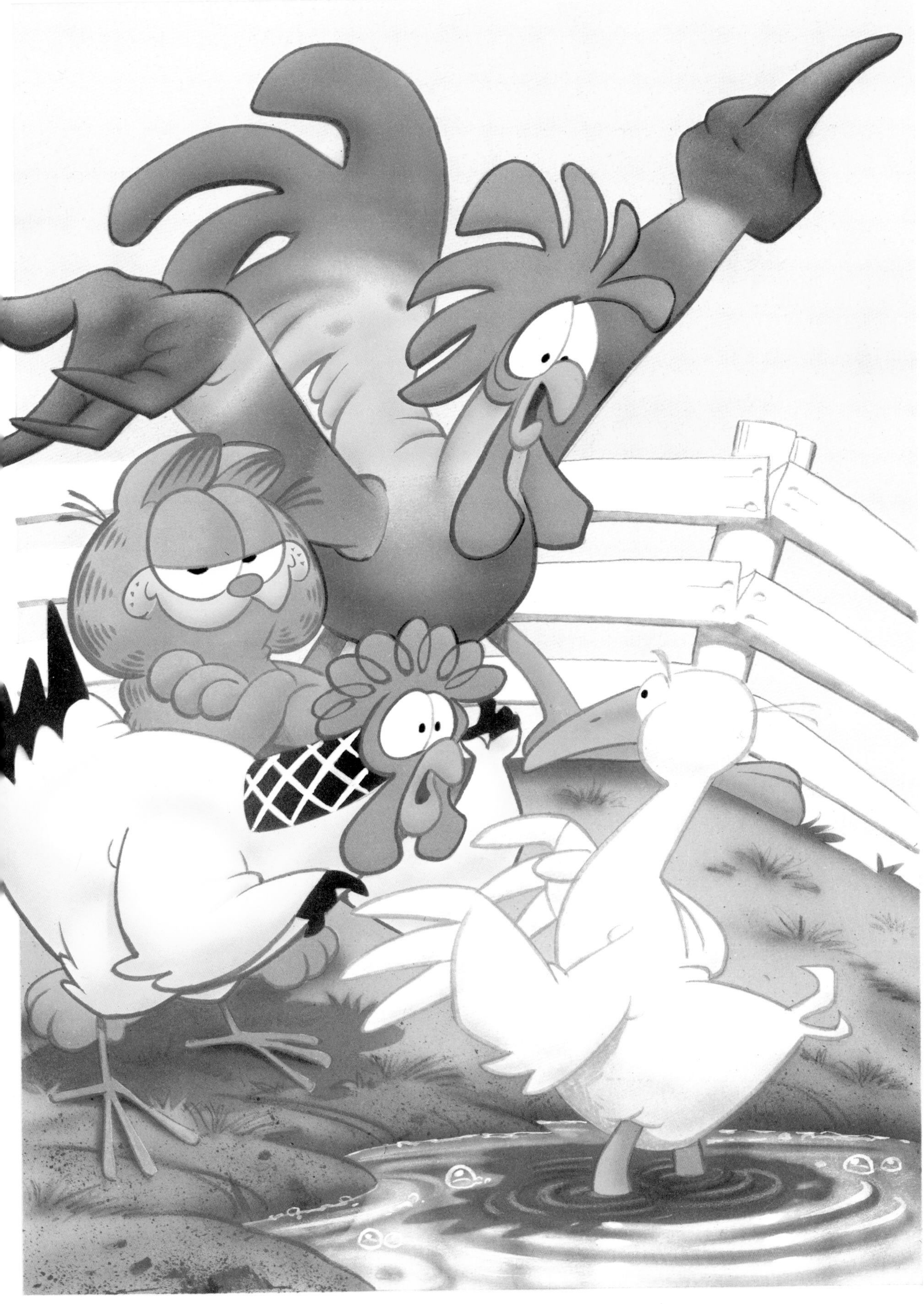

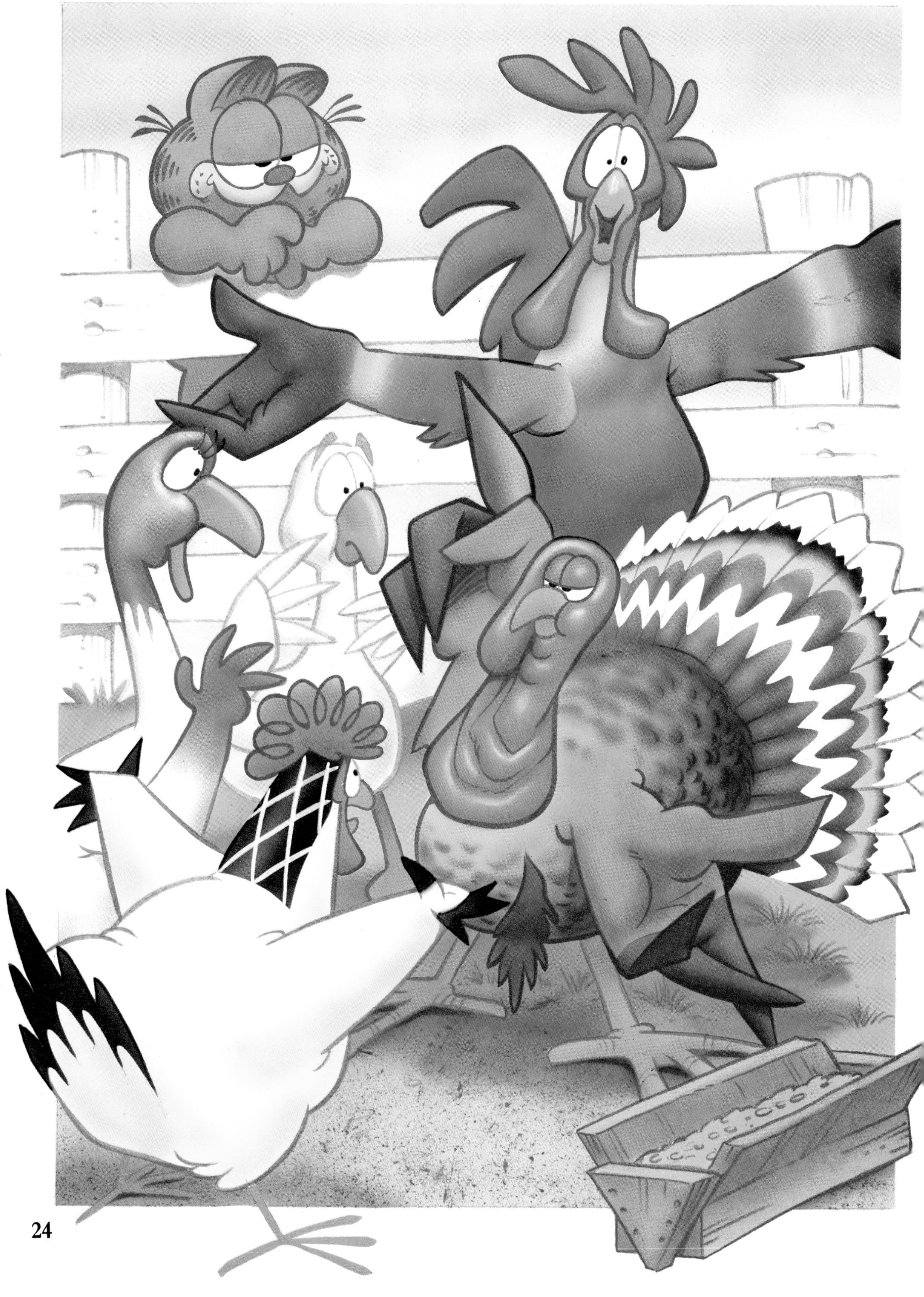

"Head for the hills!" cried Chucky Ducky. "The sky is falling!" He ran to warn the other animals, with Penny Henny and Rusty Rooster right behind.

"I'd feel guilty about this," said Garfield, "if it weren't so much fun."

Down by the lake they ran into Lucy Goosey, but fortunately no one was hurt.

"The sky is falling! The sky is falling!" shouted Penny Henny, Rusty Rooster, and Chucky Ducky at Lucy Goosey.

Lucy Goosey looked up at the sky. It was dotted with small cottonball clouds. Then she looked at the panic-stricken animals.

"Very funny," said Lucy Goosey.

"Don't you believe us?" said Penny Henny.

"I wasn't hatched yesterday," said Lucy Goosey.

"But a big piece of it squashed two hundred ducks on the next farm!" said Chucky Ducky.

"And a piece of it hit me on the head," said Penny Henny.

"You look okay to me," said Lucy Goosey.

"She's a plucky little chicken," the others replied.

Garfield saw that this goose was not so silly. "Whoa!" he said suddenly, pointing at the sky. "Did you see that?"

"Did we see what?" the animals cried.

"That big cloud just dropped like a rock," said Garfield.

"Aaaaahhhhh!" cried the animals, and they ran away, Lucy Goosey among them.

"Garfield, you're a genius," thought Garfield.

Tommy Turkey didn't know what to make of the frightened animals that came pounding toward him. "The sky is falling! The sky is falling!" they shouted. "Run for your life!"

"Don't be ridiculous," said Tommy Turkey, pointing at the sky. "The sky's right where it always was."

"Ha! That's what I used to think," said Lucy Goosey. "But a falling cloud nearly ripped my tail feathers off. And Penny Henny was struck by a piece of sky, but fortunately she recovered."

"Well, she always was a plucky little chicken," said Tommy Turkey. "But I still don't know about this."

"You mean you don't believe Penny Henny, Rusty Rooster, Chucky Ducky, Lucy Goosey, Humpty Dumpty, and Whoopty Doopty?" asked Garfield.

"Well . . . " said Tommy Turkey.

"And I guess those stories about Thanksgiving turkey are just rumors, too?" said Garfield.

"Okay, okay! I'm out of here!" said Tommy Turkey.

"Once a turkey, always a turkey," said Garfield.

The animals sped off in a cloud of feathers. But they didn't know where to go, so they just ran around in circles.

Now, it happened that Freddie Fox was passing by the farm and heard all the uproar about the sky falling. Instantly he got an idea. Trotting up to the group of animals, he said, "You're in luck, friends. I know just the place where you can hide until the disaster is over."

"Really?" said the animals with great interest.

"It's completely sky-proof," said Freddie Fox. "It even has a hot tub." What Freddie meant was that it had a pot boiling on the stove large enough to cook several fat birds.

"Let's go!" cried all the animals.

Freddie Fox led them to an old oak tree on the edge of the farm. Under its roots was a hole leading to his den.

"Step right on in," said Freddie Fox. "Plenty of room."

Garfield realized what Freddie was up to. If Penny Henny, Rusty Rooster, Chucky Ducky, Lucy Goosey, and Tommy Turkey squeezed into Freddie Fox's den, they would be safe from

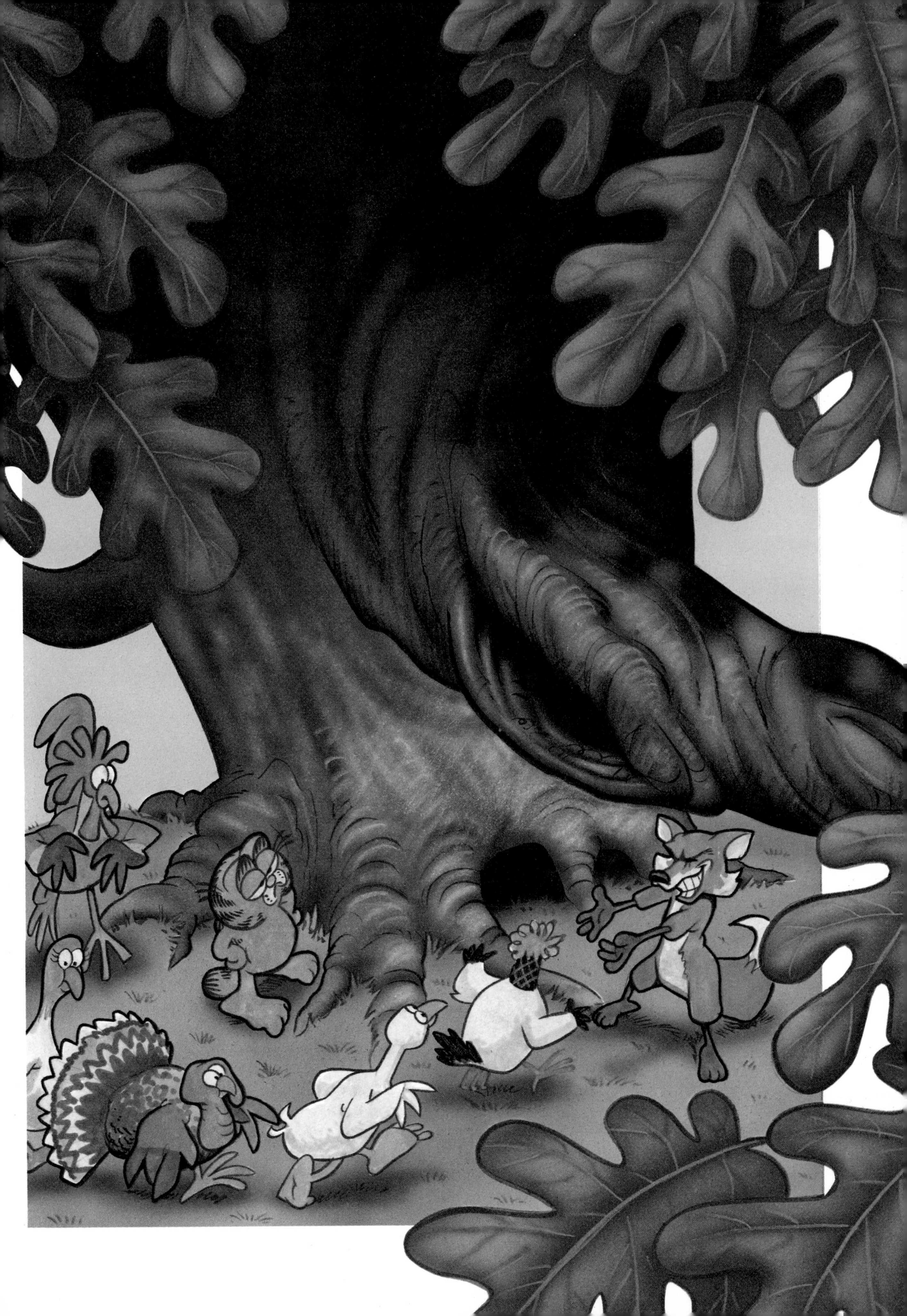

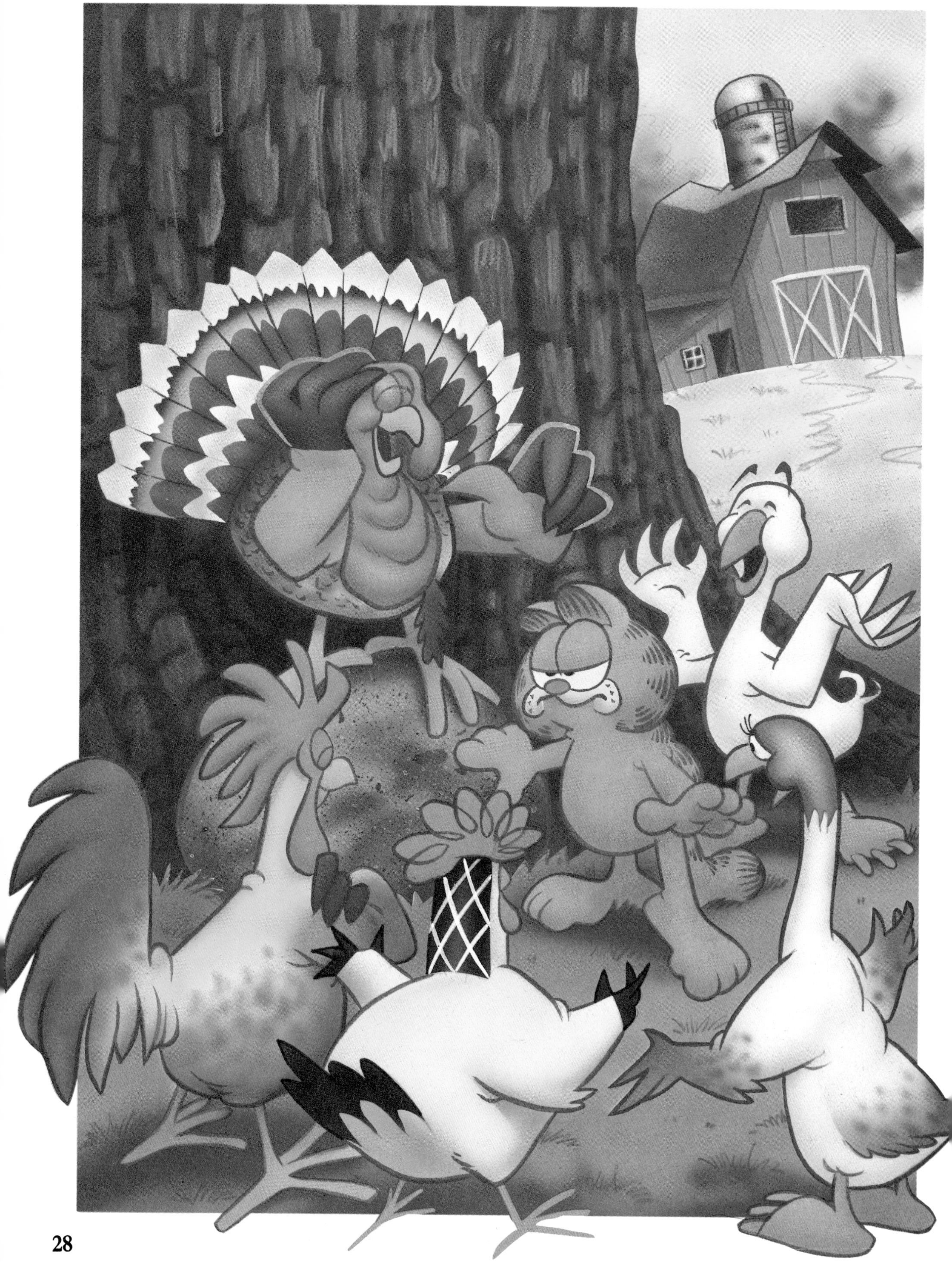

the falling sky—on Freddie's dinner table! Garfield had been enjoying his joke, but now it wasn't funny.

"Maybe those fox hunters could join us, too," said Garfield, pointing across the field.

"Out of my way, featherbrains!" cried Freddie Fox as he shoved the others aside and dove into his hole. Quickly Garfield rolled a heavy rock across the entrance. "That should help Freddie feel more secure," he said.

"But what about us?" cried Penny Henny. "Any second now a piece of sky is going to pound me to a pulp. It almost happened already, you know."

"But you got better," said Garfield.

"I'm a plucky little chicken," said Penny Henny.

"You barnyard boobs!" said Garfield. "The sky isn't falling. It never was. You got carried away, that's all."

The animals all stared at him.

"I knew that," Penny Henny said finally.

"I was just playing along," said Rusty Rooster.

"I can't believe you guys fell for that," said Chucky Ducky. "It's the oldest joke in the book."

"Of course," said Lucy Goosey. "You know, I wasn't hatched yesterday."

"I could barely keep from laughing," said Tommy Turkey.

"Well, now we can all go back home and forget about the sky falling, right?" said Garfield.

"Right," said the other animals, laughing.

"But keep an eye out for those Martians that have landed," said Garfield.

"Martians?" said the animals. "Run for your lives!"

"I'll say one thing for these barnyard fowl," observed Garfield. "They may not be bright, but they're fun!"

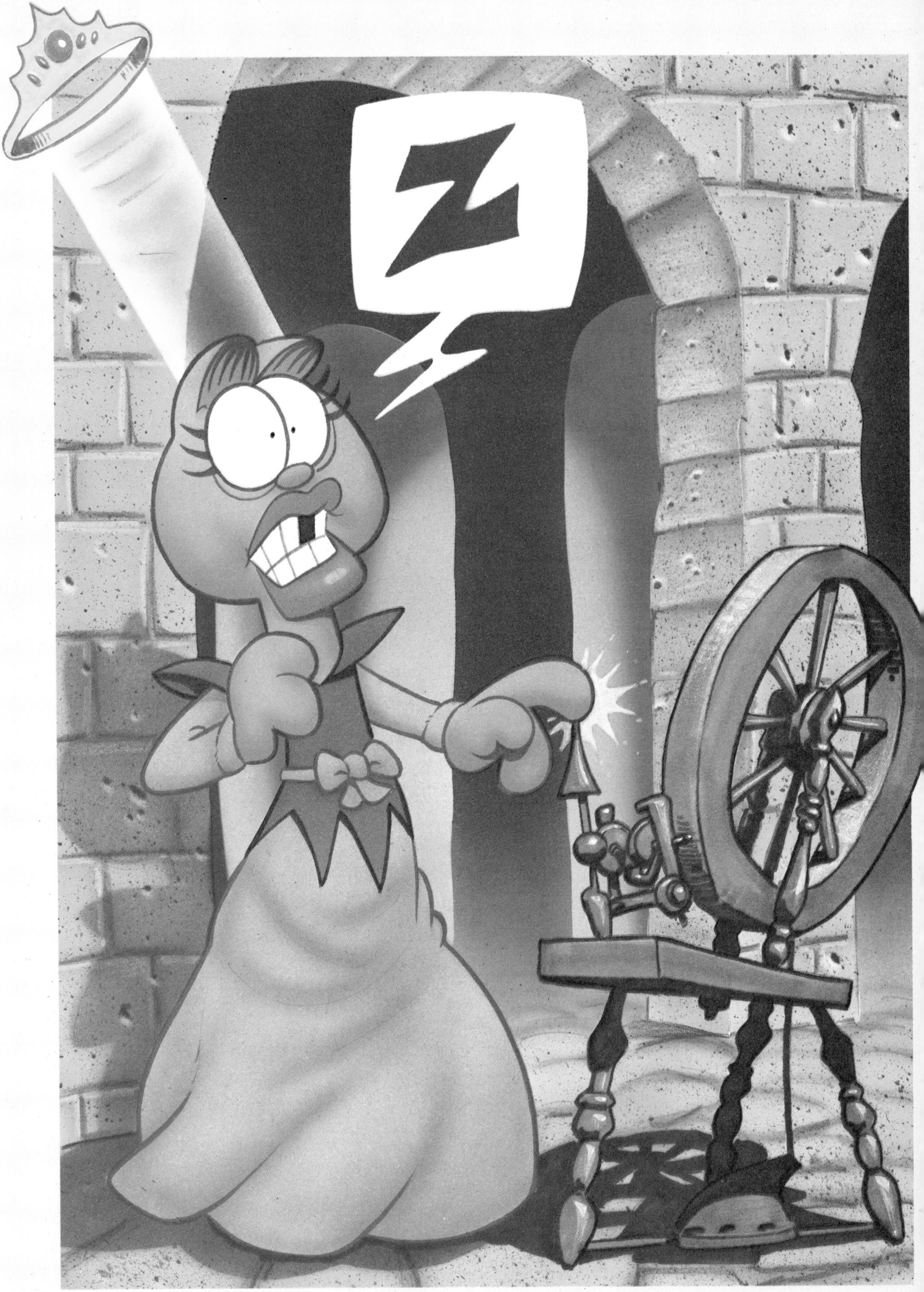
Z

Garfield and the Sleeping Beauty

Once upon a time—actually, a little more than a hundred years before that—a king and queen threw a party to celebrate the birth of their daughter. Everyone in the kingdom was invited to the party except for an evil witch. She was not invited because, after all, she was an evil witch. The witch, however, was not very understanding. In a fit of anger she put a curse on the little princess. "On the day she pricks her finger on a spinning wheel," wailed the witch, "the princess will die!"

Naturally the king and queen were upset by this news. But a good fairy offered them some comfort. "I cannot entirely undo this evil spell," said the good fairy, "but I can alter it so your daughter will not die. If she pricks her finger, she will fall into a deep sleep for one hundred years. Then she will be awakened by the kiss of a handsome prince."

The queen wasn't sure she wanted her daughter to be kissed by a stranger, but the king convinced her it was better than nothing. Then he issued a decree that all the spinning wheels in the kingdom were to be burned.

Alas, it was no use. One day Princess Arlene came upon an old spinning wheel. She touched it, pricked her finger, and fell fast asleep.

At that moment the good fairy reappeared. She put all the servants in the castle into a deep sleep, too. That way, when Princess Arlene awoke, they would be able to serve her and clean the castle, which was bound to be a bit dusty after a hundred years. To insure that no one would disturb the princess until the spell was broken, the good fairy hid the castle in a tangled mass of prickly bushes.

So Princess Arlene and everyone else in the castle slept their hundred-year sleep. One hundred years later to the day, in the kingdom next door, young Prince Garfield was training to be king. Early one morning he went out riding with his faithful companion, Sir Jon, and the royal dog, Odie.

"Don't you love the brisk morning air, my prince?" said Sir Jon.

"When I'm king, I'm going to outlaw mornings," grumbled Prince Garfield. He gulped down another flask of coffee.

"See how the dew glitters on the grass," said Sir Jon.

"And sogs up my socks," said Prince Garfield.

"I don't believe I've ever seen a more breathtaking view," said Sir Jon.

"If you don't knock it off, you're going to get a view of the royal dungeon," said Prince Garfield.

At that moment the royal dog came to a sudden halt.

"My prince," said Sir Jon, "methinks the royal hound has stumbled upon something."

"Probably his tongue," said Prince Garfield.

But Odie had stopped before a thick wall of brambles.

"Ah," said Sir Jon. "This must be that enchanted place the peasants speak of. Some say that within these thorns lies the castle of a fierce ogre."

"Well, he should trim his bushes," said Prince Garfield.

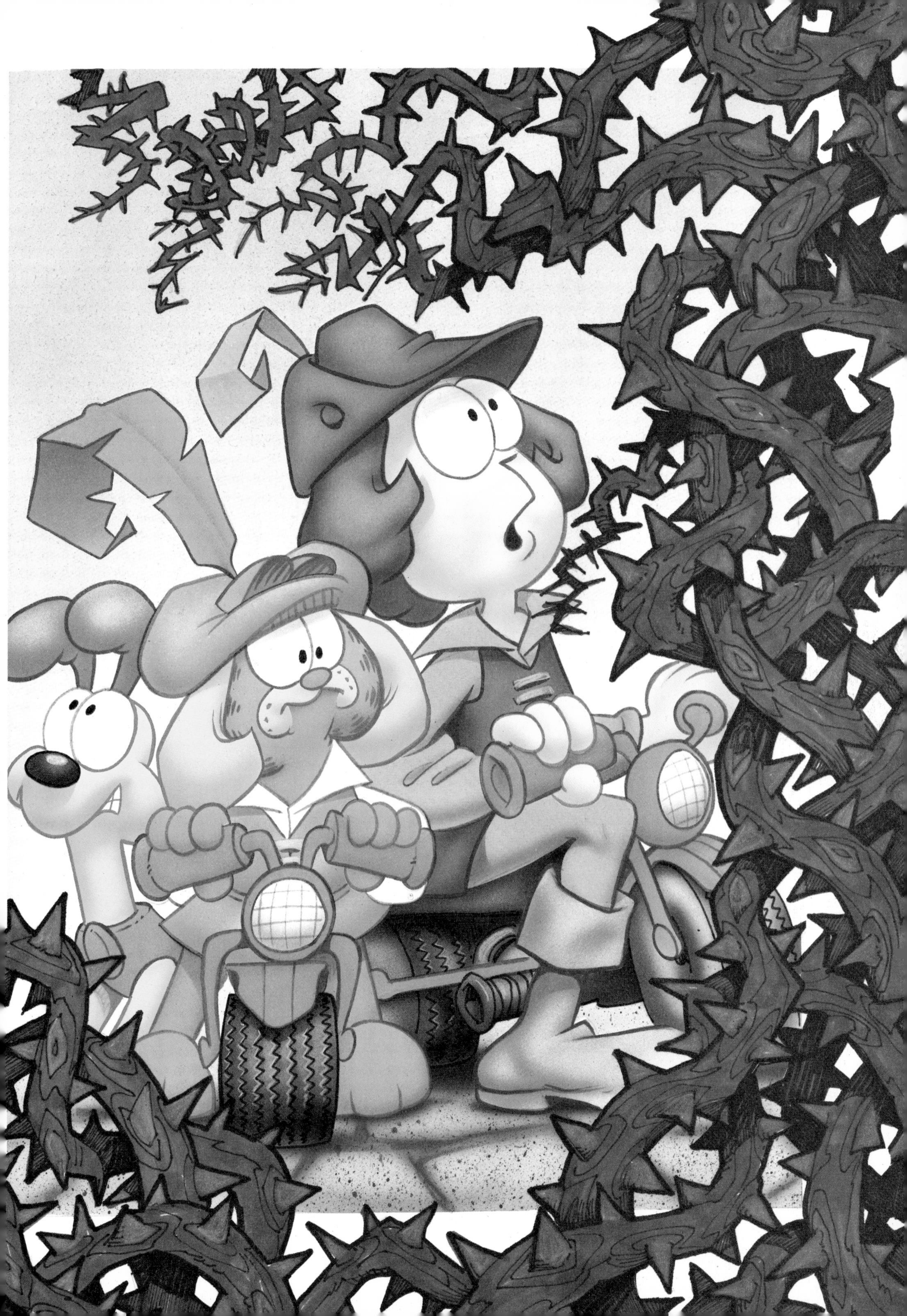

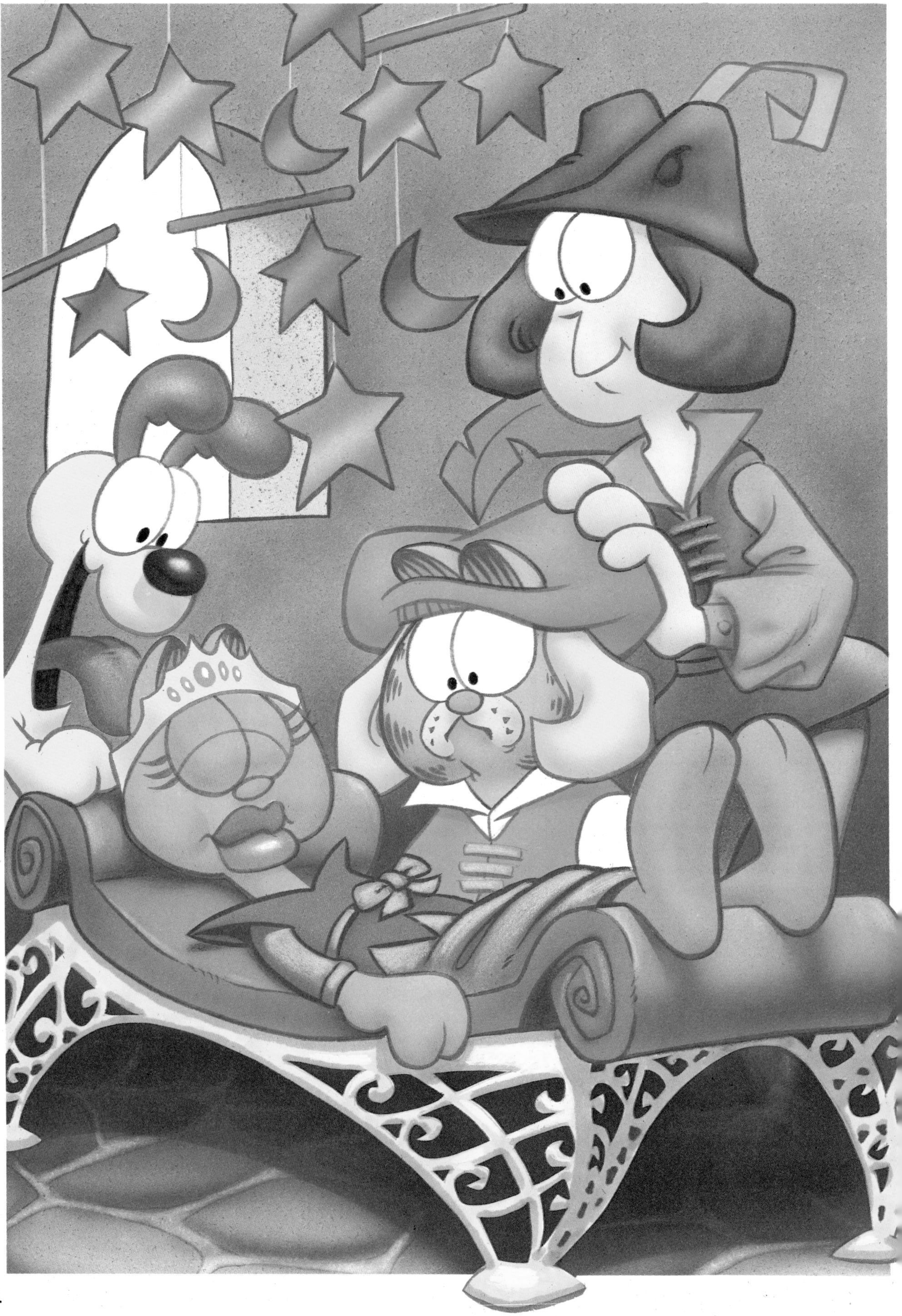

"Others claim that this is the castle of a beautiful princess who sleeps under an evil witch's spell, waiting for a handsome prince to awaken her with a kiss," said Sir Jon.

"That's nice," said Prince Garfield. "Now let's go back to our castle. I've run out of coffee."

But Odie was still nosing around the brambles. Suddenly they parted, revealing a winding path.

"Shall we enter, my prince?" said Sir Jon.

Prince Garfield hesitated. What if this really was the castle of an ogre? Getting eaten by an ogre was way, way down on his list of fun things. Still, he was a prince, and finding a sleeping princess was a princely thing to do.

"You first," said Prince Garfield.

The brambles grew so thick around the path that Prince Garfield and Sir Jon couldn't see the sky. But soon they came to the courtyard of a large castle.

"Look!" said Sir Jon, gasping. "There are servants sleeping everywhere."

"Just like at our castle," said Prince Garfield.

"Then the legend must be true," said Sir Jon. "This must be the castle of the Sleeping Beauty. We must find her."

With the royal dog leading the way, they raced through the castle. Finally, at the top of a tall tower, in a room hung with beautiful ruby and emerald stars, they found the princess sleeping peacefully on a bed of gold.

Sir Jon looked at Prince Garfield. "My prince, you must kiss her and break the spell."

Prince Garfield looked at the sleeping Princess Arlene. The truth was, she wasn't exactly a Sleeping Beauty. She was more like a Sleeping Not-Too-Terrible-Looking. "It seems a shame to wake her," said Prince Garfield. "I wouldn't mind a hundred-year nap every now and then."

"Stop stalling, my prince," said Sir Jon anxiously.

"After one hundred years, her breath must be pretty bad," said Prince Garfield. "I think I'd rather kiss an ogre."

"You're a disgrace to all princes," said Sir Jon.

"All right, I'll do it," said Prince Garfield.

But before Prince Garfield had a chance, Odie jumped up and gave Arlene a great big sloppy lick.

"Yech!" Arlene said, shivering. Slowly she opened her eyes and saw Prince Garfield.

"Oh, my fair prince," said Arlene as she gazed into his eyes. "You have freed me." Then the princess smiled.

"Boy, that witch must have put a curse on your mouth," said Prince Garfield. "You could slap a hockey puck through the gap between your two front teeth."

"And you, my prince," said the enraged princess, "look as if you have swallowed a cannonball!"

"Seems like somebody got up on the wrong side of the castle," said Prince Garfield.

"Your majesties, please!" said Sir Jon. "This story is supposed to have a happy ending."

Prince Garfield and Princess Arlene looked at each other.

"All right, all right," said Prince Garfield. "I guess we could give it a try." He sent Odie to wake up the rest of the people in the castle. Prince Garfield and Princess Arlene had the blessing of the king and queen to marry, which they did the next week.

The prince and princess moved to Prince Garfield's kingdom, where they soon ruled wisely as king and queen. For his services, Odie was awarded the Order of the Golden Flea Collar. Sir Jon was named Royal Adviser for as long as he promised not to make King Garfield go on any more early-morning rides. And everyone napped happily ever after.

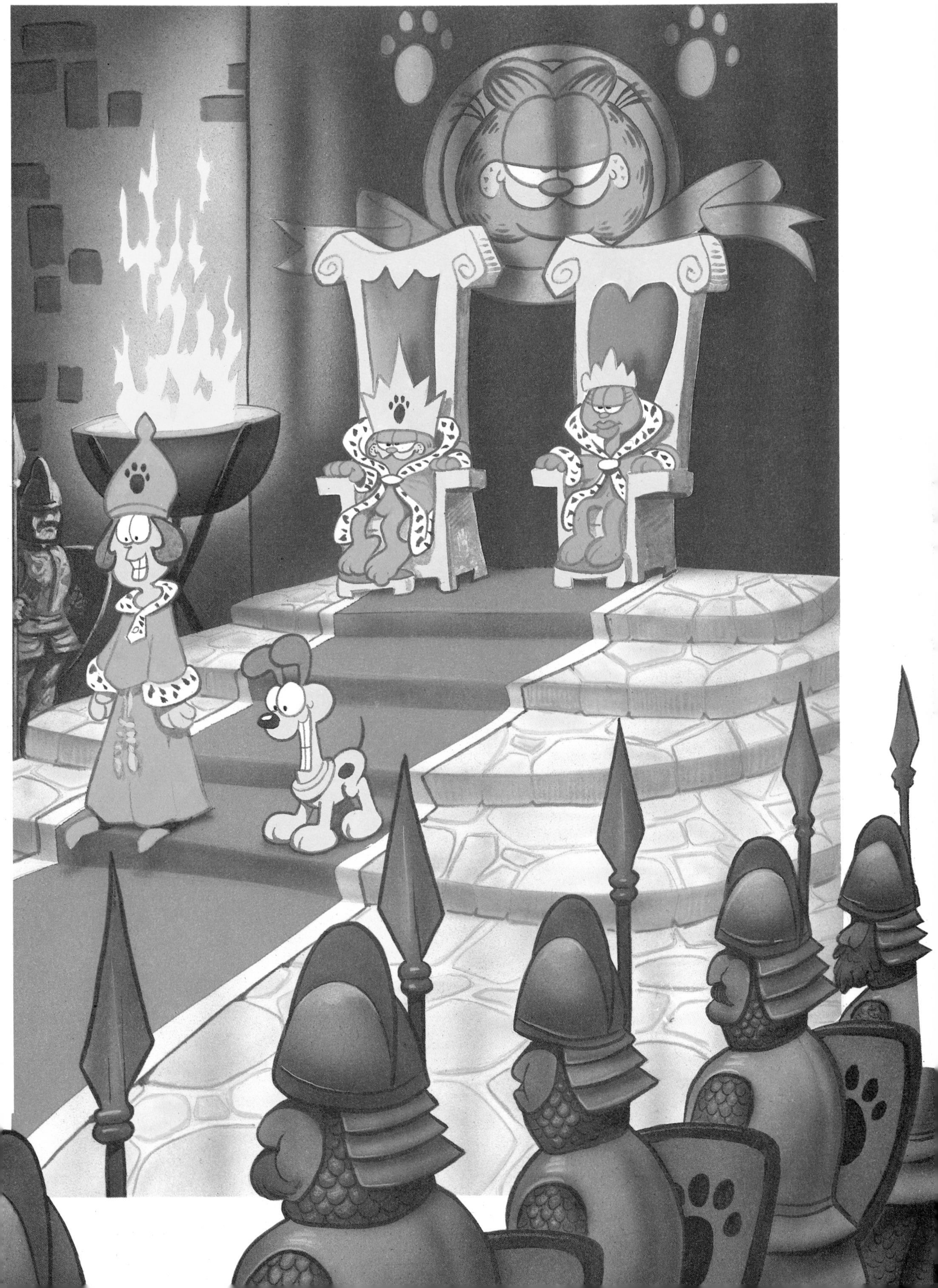

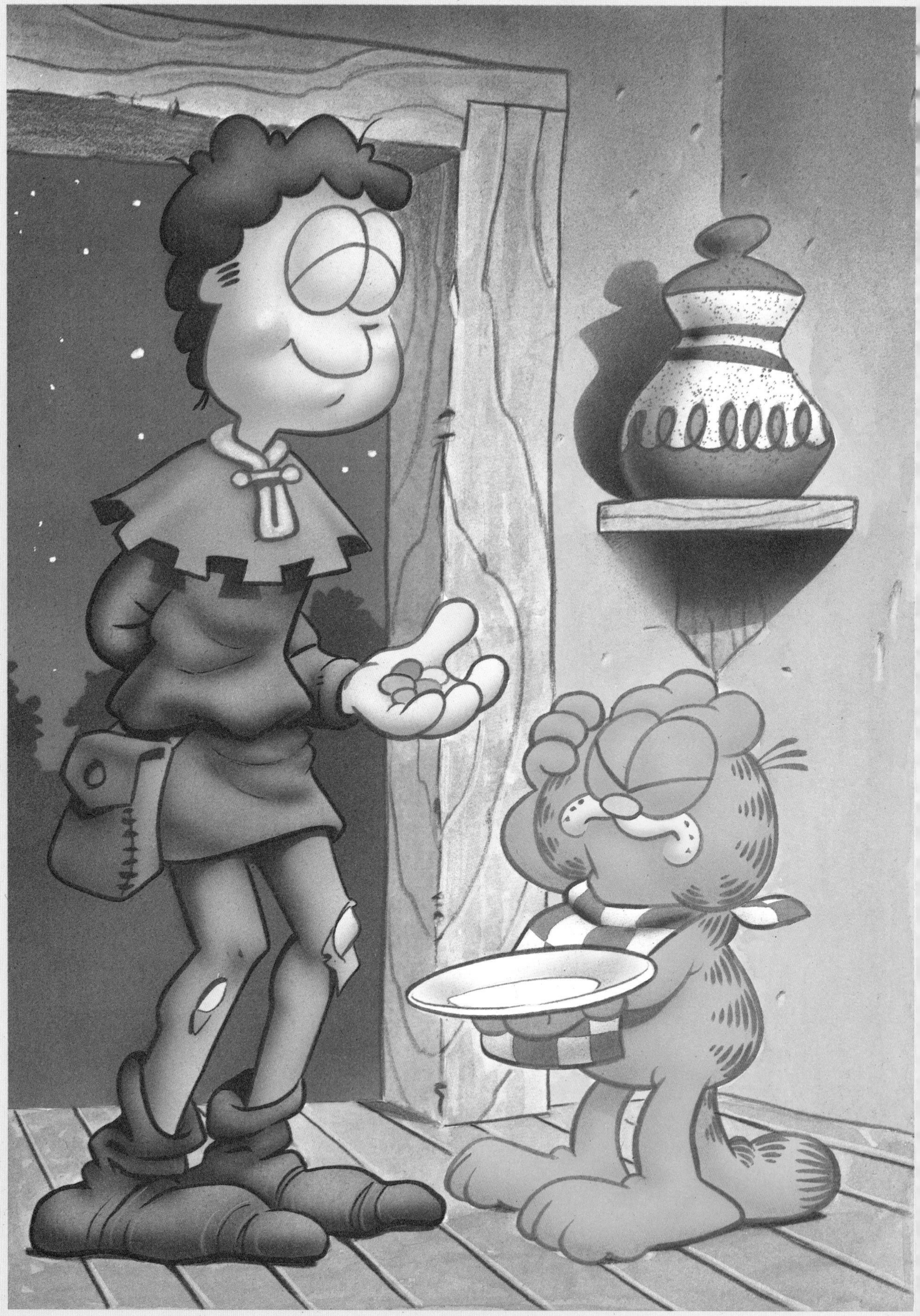

Garfield and the Beanstalk

Once upon a time there was a farmer named Jon, who had a dog named Odie and a cat named Garfield. It hadn't rained for a long time, so the crops didn't grow. Jon became very poor and did not have enough food. This was especially difficult because Garfield liked to eat all day, every day. Finally Jon decided that there were too many mouths to feed.

"I hate to say this," he told Garfield and Odie, "but I'm going to have to sell one of you. But I just can't choose. Would either one of you step forward and volunteer?"

Garfield realized that he had to take action. So he set his jaw, stuck out his chest, and shoved Odie forward.

"You're a brave little dog, Odie," said Jon.

"See if you can't trade him for a steak," said Garfield.

The next day a sad Jon took Odie to the market. When Jon returned that evening, Garfield was waiting at the door with a napkin around his neck and a plate in his hands.

"What did you get? Gimme, gimme, gimme!" said Garfield.

Jon held out his hand.

"Beans?" said Garfield. "You come back with five lousy beans? Couldn't you at least get some hot dogs, too?"

"These are magic beans," said Jon.

"Then let them turn themselves into a six-course dinner."

"The man who gave me these said I should plant them and see what happens," said Jon.

"This is what's going to happen," said Garfield. He grabbed the beans from Jon's hand and tossed them into his mouth. But the beans were hard and did not taste very good. "Yech!" said Garfield, spitting the beans out the window.

So that night Jon and Garfield went to bed hungry again.

"I wonder if I could trade Jon for a decent meal," grumbled Garfield.

When he awoke the next morning, he found an incredible surprise. The beans he had spit out had grown overnight into a giant beanstalk that reached up to the clouds.

"It's a good thing I didn't eat those beans," said Garfield, "or I'd be having some tummy ache!"

Garfield looked at the beanstalk again. "I guess they *were* magic beans," he thought. "Maybe the beanstalk goes to a magic land where there is a lot of magic food. Too bad there isn't an elevator. I'll have to climb."

Up and up Garfield climbed, until finally his head poked through the clouds. Before his eyes loomed an enormous castle. "Any place that big must have a huge kitchen," he thought. "Breakfast, here I come!"

Using his stomach as a guide, Garfield soon found the kitchen. And it *was* huge! Best of all, so was the food. Garfield feasted his eyes on eggs as big as houses and sweet rolls that looked like snow-capped mountains. There were strips of bacon so long he could barely see the ends of them, while a huge cup contained an ocean of coffee. "This is paradise," Garfield said with a sigh. "I'm never leaving."

But just as Garfield was about to stuff a two-ton sausage into his mouth, he heard *Boom! Boom!* heading his way.

As the door crashed open, Garfield ducked behind some

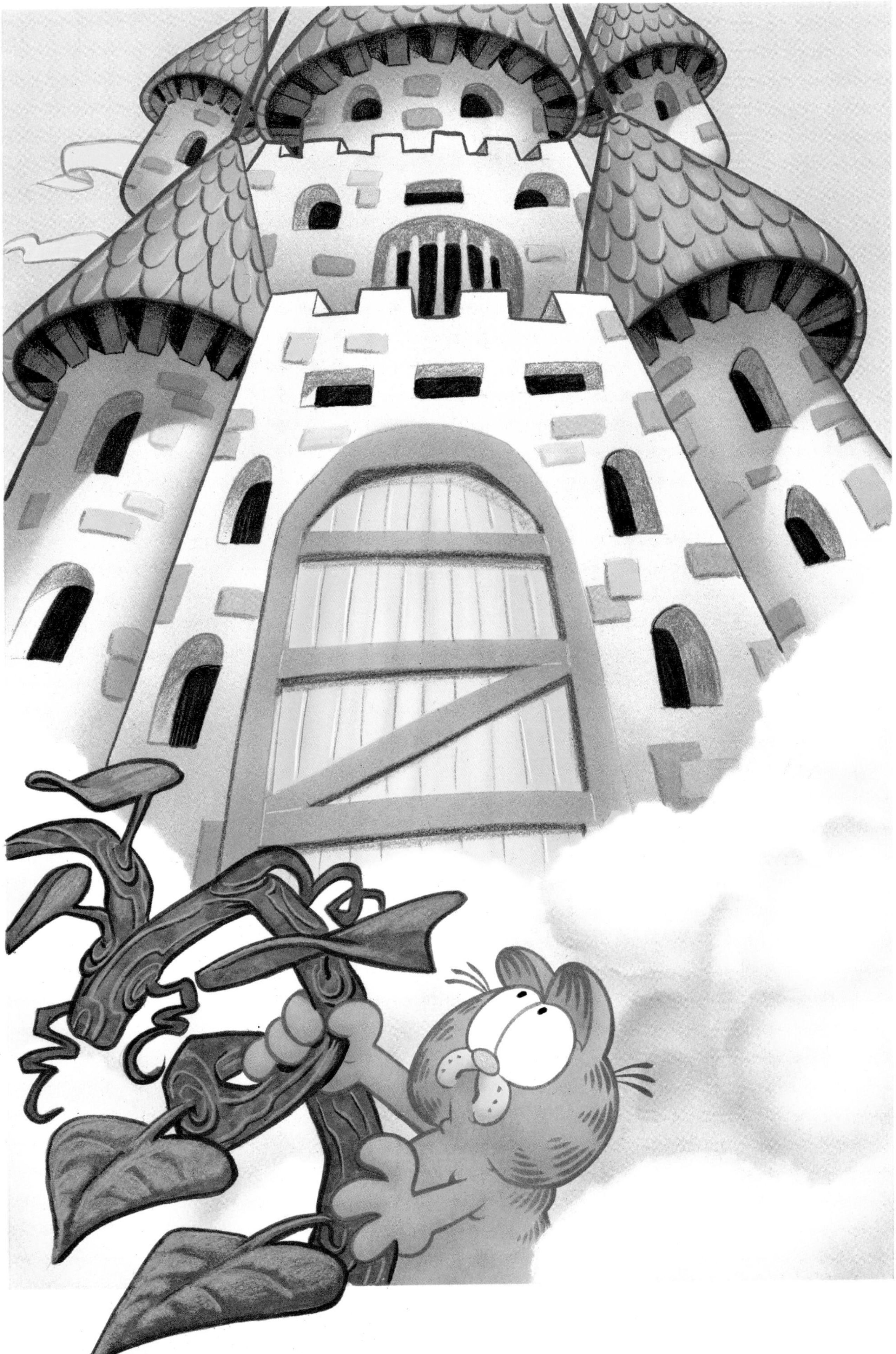

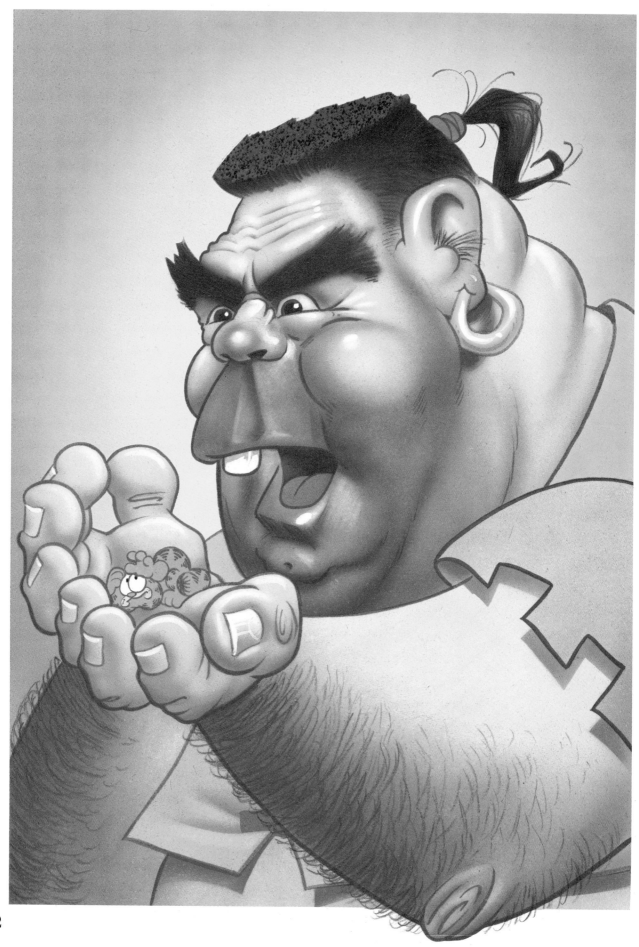

blueberries. In walked a fierce-looking giant who seemed nearly as tall as the beanstalk and more than twice as wide as Jon's farm. "Boy, this guy must have eaten all his vegetables when he was a kid," thought Garfield.

The giant stopped and looked around. He sniffed the air, his giant nose twitching. Then he sniffed some more until— *Aaahhh-choooooo!* He let loose a sneeze that shook the room like an avalanche of blueberries!

"Fee-fi-fo-fat!" said the giant. "I smell the blood of an overweight cat!"

"Who are you calling overweight, Blimpo?" said Garfield. "You've got fat cells the size of a small planet."

"Aha!" shouted the giant, plunging his fist into the pile of blueberries. One by one he picked them out and tossed them away, until all that remained in his palm was a very round orange-and-black berry named Garfield.

"Here's a tasty little morsel," said the giant, squinting at Garfield through watery eyes. "I'd eat you now, but I'm trying not to eat between meals. You'll be great on my spinach salad at lunch. Everything tastes good when you're on a diet." The giant sniffed and rubbed his eyes.

Then the giant put Garfield into a small glass jar with airholes punched in the lid. He set the jar on the kitchen table and walked into the next room. Through the doorway Garfield watched him take a large sack from his pocket and toss it onto a table. The sack came open, spilling out dozens of enormous gold coins.

"Wow!" said Garfield. "If we had just one of those coins, we'd be rich enough to send out for pizza every night. We could sell the farm and buy a nice condo next door to a lasagna factory. We might even have enough left over to buy back Odie."

Of course, that was only a dream, now that Garfield was on the giant's lunch menu. He was sorry that he wouldn't get a chance to say good-bye to Jon. He was sorrier for the way he had treated Odie. And he was sorriest of all that he still hadn't had any breakfast. "There's nothing worse than being eaten on an empty stomach," thought Garfield. "I guess I might as well take one last nap."

A short time later Garfield was awakened by the sound of something licking the jar. It was Odie, and next to him was Jon. "I must be dreaming," Garfield said.

"We've come to rescue you, Garfield," whispered Jon.

"Arf!" Odie barked.

"Quiet!" said Jon. "We don't want to wake the giant." Garfield could see the giant sleeping in the next room.

"We've got to get you out of this jar," said Jon. Very carefully Jon and Odie tipped the jar on its side. But the table wasn't level, and the jar began to roll.

"Whoa!" shouted Garfield as he bounced around the inside of the jar. Odie and Jon chased after the jar, but it was rolling too fast for them to stop. They watched in horror as the jar shattered on the kitchen floor.

Jon and Odie peered over the edge of the table. "Are you all right, Garfield?" shouted Jon.

"I'll get you for this, Jon," said Garfield, dazed, but all in one piece.

Unfortunately the crash had awakened the giant! He came roaring into the kitchen, crying, "Fee-fi-fo-fog! I smell a man and a dim-witted dog."

Garfield, Jon, and Odie ran as fast as they could toward the beanstalk, with the giant thundering right behind them.

"It's no use," said Jon, gasping for air. "We'll never outrun that giant. This is the end, boys."

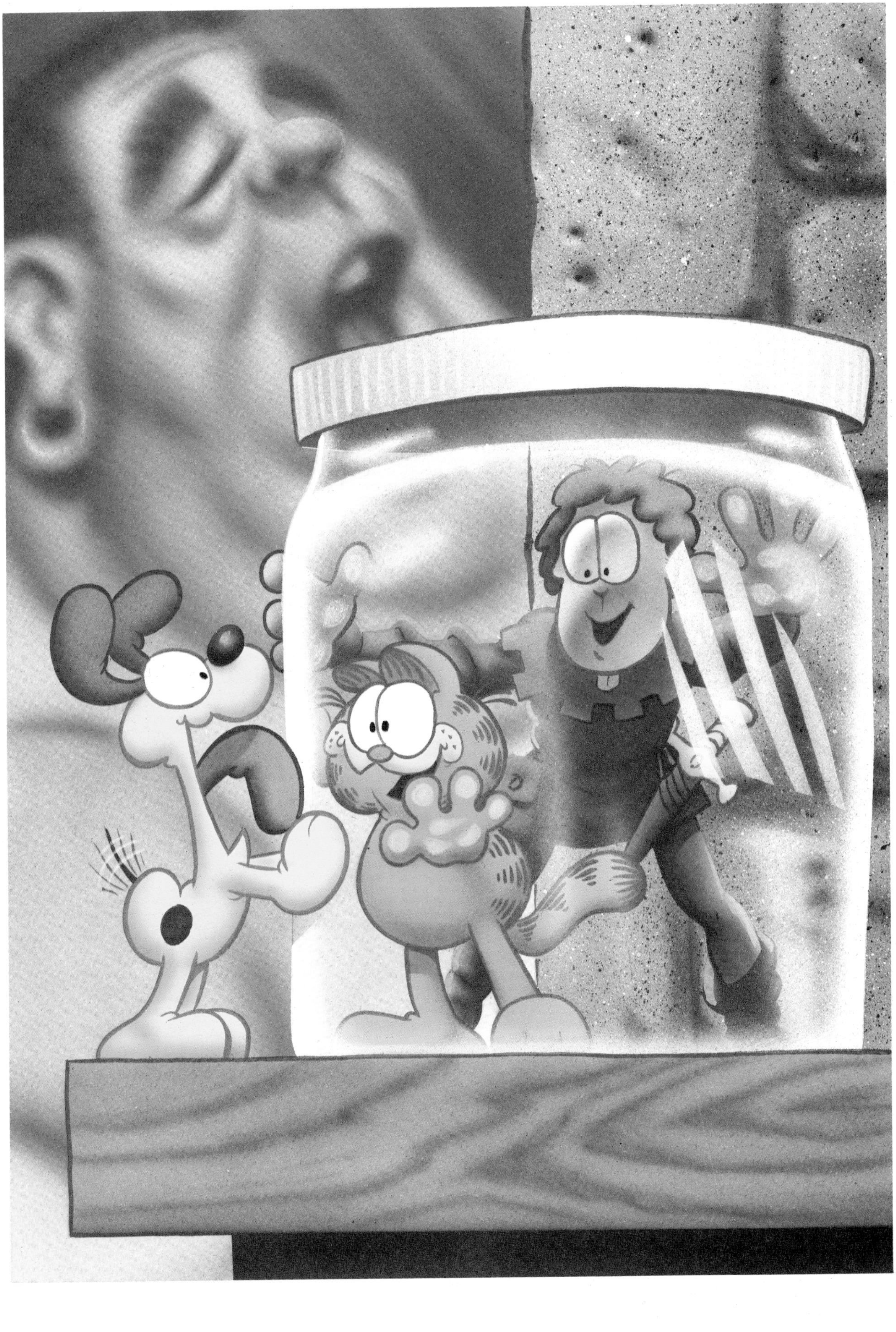

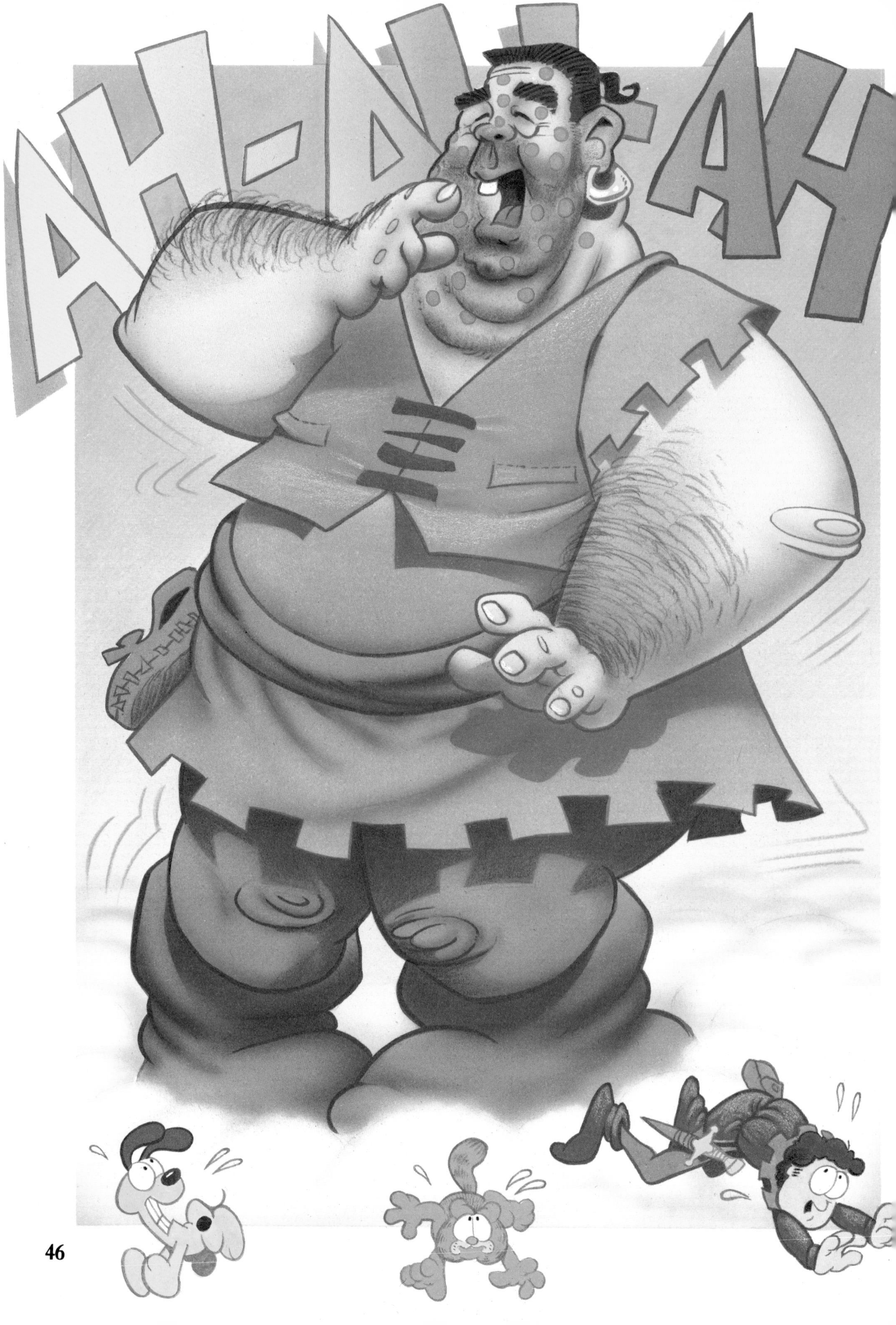
AH-AH-AH

"Maybe not," said Garfield. "There is one last thing I can try—shedding." In seconds the ground around them was covered with a carpet of cat hair.

"Gave up, did you?" roared the giant. "Good!" As he stretched out his giant hand toward the three helpless adventurers, a strange look came over his face. And then he began to sneeze and sneeze and sneeze. It sounded like thousands of firecrackers going off. At the same time, big pink splotches popped out on the giant's face like hot-air balloons. The giant began to wobble and weave, until finally he fell over with a tremendous crash!

"Just as I thought," said Garfield. "This giant is very, very, very allergic to cat hair."

"You saved us, Garfield!" said Jon.

"We're even," said Garfield.

Before they climbed back down the beanstalk, they took three gold coins from the giant's pocket, rolled them to the edge of the cloud, and pushed them off. Then they climbed down. With a chain saw Jon cut down the beanstalk, in case the giant had any friends who weren't allergic to cat hair.

That night Jon explained how Odie had run away from the man who had given Jon the magic beans. When they saw the beanstalk, they figured that Garfield, being a curious cat, must have climbed it. So they climbed up after him to see if he was all right.

That day marked the beginning of a better life for all of them. The gold coins had buried themselves in Jon's property. Jon became the owner of the richest gold mine in the country. Odie became a rich man's pampered dog. And Garfield became the owner of the biggest lasagna factory in the country—which filled his heart with joy and his tummy with all the lasagna he could ever dream about eating.